SOCIAL CHANGE
IN EUROPE

SOME DEMOGRAPHIC CONSEQUENCES

SOCIAL CHANGE
IN EUROPE

SOME DEMOGRAPHIC CONSEQUENCES

EDITED BY

B. W. FRIJLING

LEIDEN
E. J. BRILL
1973

ISBN 90 04 03548 6

75 - 69 16

CONTENTS

Sj. GROENMAN, Social Change in Europe: Some Consequences for
Demography 1

Egon SZABADY, The Social and Demographic Changes of Hungarian
Society During the Last 25 Years 13

Ivan STEFANOV, Socio-Economic Changes and Internal Migration in
Bulgaria 38

Egon SZABADY, Mortality Trends in the Socialist Countries of Eastern
Europe after World War II 54

John A. JACKSON, Migration and Social Change in Europe 67

Jan TROST, Marriage-Rates in Sweden 80

Guillaume WUNSCH, Recent Trends of Nuptiality in Some European
Countries. A Demographic Analysis 91

Bernhard FRIJLING, Some Notes on the Changing Fertility in Europe and
the Study of it 120

Hein G. MOORS, Family Planning Patterns: An Experiment in Describing
Modern Fertility Trends 128

Social Change in Europe:
Some Consequences for Demography

SJ. GROENMAN

Utrecht

I. Introduction

IT is no use to ask whether or not demography is a discipline in itself and where eventually its borders might be located. There are only very few, if any, elements of a specifically demographic nature. As soon as these elements are taken as subjects for scientific study we see that the borders are rapidly vanishing. The area of study is expanding more and more, and it seems to be boundless. In fact, the safest definition of demography is simply: what demographers deal with. The contributions to this volume offer clear illustrations to this statement. For this reason it seems appropriate to make some comments upon my simple operational definition.

Demography, whatever may be its circumscription, somehow deals with numbers and changes in numbers of human aggregates. The size of an aggregate (group, category, collectivity) is as a matter of fact influenced by entries and departures. For the human population on earth this means only by birth and by death. There is no other possibility to join humanity than by birth. For parts of it there are better changes. You may get access to a political party by your own arbitrary decision, or you may be accepted as a member of a higher status group by achievement; a religious denomination is not only enlarged by birth but also by conversion; an urban or rural community may grow in number as an effect of migration. The family of Man however has no other possibility of growth than by the excess of birth over death.

Now, demographers are interested in birth and death. They extend their interest to the size of the family and to marriage, both being social institutions and belonging to the domain of the disciplines of sociology and law. It is quite normal, in our opinion, that demographers investigate the motivations behind intra-marital procreation, or that they study the motives for marrying or not marrying, for marrying early or postponing the marriage. Numbers or changes in numbers being the score of demography, the interest in marriage and family is not self-evident, although we all know that most children in our society are born within families under the rule of marriage. If demographers try to find patterns for the procreative behaviour of mankind, it is, however, not correct to take the date of the marriage-contract as a starting-point.

This date may be dependent on tradition, income or housing possibilities, whilst sexual intercourse still necessary for procreation in this not brave old world from old times on, can begin earlier. Once the demographers are interested in procreation patterns; they will be tempted to undertake research into dating and courtship, into the choice of wedding-partners, into the social position of the woman, especially into female labour. One may wonder whether all those studies belong to demography. Of course, kissing and courting may have a relation to marriage and procreation, as have "woman's two roles"; but are these genuine demographic subjects?

A consensus seems to exist about migration as a demographic subject. At close examination, however, this consensus is not a matter of course. What is the meaning of migration? People migrating leave the social surroungings somewhere on earth they are used to and they enter other surroundings of a more or less different kind. We may comment here that a man or woman leaving a religious group and entering another one change their social milieu, too, as do climbers on the social ladder. Why should demography be interested in the motives for migration and why not in the shift in religious conviction or in career-making? I do not think there is a satisfactory answer. Maybe one might answer that migration figures belong to the so-called vital statistics, registered by states, provinces and communities and therefore easily accessible Moreover, they play a part in the realm of physical planning, where social scientists and, among them, demographers in several countries have been employed for decades and decades. The emphasis on all sorts of planning for spatial entities like states and communities, and the importance of migration data in the planning process within these entities is, of course, no motive to include migration within the activity (or discipline) of demography. States, districts or communities are social, collective units among other things. Migration is merely one kind of mobility from one social milieu to another, and it is arbitrary to earmark it as a demographic phenomenon in contrast with political or religious transitons, or with moving on the social ladder. All these variations of mobility have their own characteristic motivation and adjustment, all of them influence numbers of aggregates.

The foregoing is not a plea for changing the traditional behaviour of demographers. It is not very important by what discipline or by which qualified people the problems of society are studied. What matters is that they are in effect, studied. The only reason for elaborating, in this introduction, on the difficulty of drawing satisfactory limits to the domain of demography is to make clear that in this volume under the cover of demography very different subjects come to the fore or at least are dealt with.

II. Demography as a field for comparisons

The comparative character of demography is evident. Of course there are many studies that are undertaken without the purpose to compare but simply for the sake of more knowledge about a specific subject. A not very sophisticated study on the growth of the population of a community, however, includes, quite naturally, comparative elements; index figures are typically comparative by nature; the problem of ageing per definitionem demands a comparative approach. The demographer studying the curves of birth rate and death rate often wonders whether the trends he observes may be found elsewhere. He is not surprised to detect that the "babyboom" after World War II was not unique for one European country, e.g. the Netherlands, that this phenomenon could be perceived in several countries involved in this war. If he has reason to believe that the differences in birth rate, which for years and years have been negatively correlated to income level in Western Europe, show the tendency to a positive correlation in one country (in the beginning of the thirties already in Sweden) he is eager to find other countries-comparable with that country-where the same tendency may be demonstrated. The demographer is inclined to suppose that certain countries or communities are still in a stage of demographic development already left by others. Family planning and birth control began in certain social circles and regions (not necessarily urban areas) and spread to other milieus. Leads and lags are concepts appealing to the demographer. In a period in which birth control becomes quite normal some religious groups may lag behind. The communication process however, between people of different religious convictions, between local communities or between countries, promotes a levelling of differences. What was introduced by relatively small groups found its way to all parts of society, at least in most countries of Europe.

In the light of what has been said here it is no wonder that demography is in search of demographic patterns, and that the hypothesis has been made that the same order of patterns may be discerned with different social aggregates. Several patterns are circulating within the literature. There is for instance the townbound move caused by industrialization, followed by a sub-urbanization process starting with the higher income brackets and "going down" to the lower classes. Already about 1880 E. G. Ravenstein [1] found that the urbanization process took place in stages: from village to near-by town, from there to a bigger center. Stefanow's contribution to this volume gives proof that this process, occuring already in great parts of Western Europe in the former century and still going on untill recently, is now a conspicious phenomenon in a country like Bulgaria. The countries of Eastern Europe, as may be concluded from the articles of Stefanow and Szabady, show developments the people in Western Europe are very familiar with. In the East European countries the problem of the smallest hamlets and villages threatened by total depopulation is now actual, too. Regional planning may offer a number of these settlements new functions as residential areas or recreation resorts. What was accelerated by the very rapid social development within the socialist countries, i.e. by planned industrialization, at a slower speed manifested itself in the West European countries, beginning at an earlier date.

There are, of course, more examples of patterns of demographic development detected by demographers. Malthus himself, pleading for moral restraint, harked back to an old, wide-spread pattern of non-marriage and delay of marriage existing in rural areas and among craftsmen in towns. There are lots of theories about the relation between age of marriage and birth rate and authors like Hajnal, Ryder, Matras, Hofstee and many others have tried to interpret the figures they had at hand by means of the construction of patterns. [2]

I will confine myself in this contribution to comments on two hypothetical patterns of a demographic or semi-demographic character dealing directly or indirectly with fertility. This does not mean that the foregoing summing up of suggested patterns was exhaustive. A well-known general pattern e.g. is the stage of "the demographic gap" showing a declining death rate while the birth rate is still very high, a pattern quite common in a number of developing countries. This pattern "ought" to be followed by a rather sharp decline of the birth rate after strong mental barriers have been overcome.

III. Two examples of demographic patterns

The interesting thing in this example is that it shows that it is unnatural to assume that Eastern Europe lags behind in all respects of demography. Perhaps it takes the lead this time.

The example concerns the employment of women. I realize that this subject is not as demographic as are birth and death or even marriage, but as I pointed out already in my introduction, the limits of what is demography are not very relevant. It is anyhow justified to suggest that birth rate may have a relation with the employment of women, especially the employment of married women.

In Hungary the employment of women has increased considerable. Before World War II the majority of the employed women was unmarried, widows and divorced included. Now the majority of the women earners is married. This shift brought about that now nearly two thirds of the female population belong to the gainfully employed, the figure in 1949 being only one third. In the total labour force women numbered 30% in 1949, and now 40%.

As a good demographer Szabady has tried to locate this development within a classification scheme. He discerns three types of solutions for the problem married women are faced with. Married women play their role as mothers and, in our society, also as house-keepers. On the other hand, an increasing number of married women have full-time or part-time jobs. The easiest solution of course is not to play the two roles at the same time: in some periods, i.e. during several years, they abstain from employment outside the family, in other periods they take up a job. A more difficult solution is to combine the two roles during the same period. Widows and divorced women with children to be taken care of had long since been forced to choose this solution. Combining the roles, at the same moment, within a complete, not a broken family, presupposes the configuration of quite a number of factors of variable strength. The emancipation of women and the acceptance of strict family-planning, which implies a restriction of the number of children, the necessity to increase the family resources in order to reach a modest or a comfortable level of living, the interplay of supply and demand on the labour market, the emphasis on a national effort to increase production and the coming into existence of the welfare state (crèches and kindergartens), all combine to create a situation where married women may be motivated to enter the labour force. In some countries also fiscal elements are important in the decision whether or not a married woman may take up a job. The social and economic policy of the government is of course of great importance. We see here that demography touches quite a lot of fields belonging to economy, sociology, psychology, law and political science. The problem mentioned by Szabady also has relations to my second example concerning marriage (see below).

I now come to the patterns pointed out by the Hungarian author.

1. Within the first type come those countries where the rate of the female workers between 20 and 55 years – the overwhelming majority married – reaches a height of approximately 60–70%. Examples are the East European countries, such as Bulgaria, Poland and Romania.
   In this pattern the two roles have been combined in the same period of marriage.
2. Within the second group those countries can be ranked where most of the women earners are in their early twenties. The rate of married women in the labour force after that stage falls down and remains low in the following periods. To this category belong e.g. Belgium, the Netherlands and Italy.
3. Within the third pattern fall those countries where, following the peak of employment shows a temporary decrease. Toward the end of the thirties, however, it begins to increase and reaches another peak after.
   Examples are the U.S.A., the U.K. and France.

The two last patterns offer the solution to the roles conflict of the married woman by a separation in time. They are principally different, however. The second pattern is the traditional one for those parts of the population since female labour was accepted where there was no financial necessity of a higher income. It is clear that in the nineteenth century this pattern was not applicable to the working-class. The second pattern is restricted to the middle class. As prosperity rose, the pattern found its way, at least in Western Europe, to great parts of the working class. The interesting fact is that among labourers in Western Europe now there is often a rather strong resistance to labour of married women. In former generations the wives of the labourers had to work outside the family in order to remain above the poverty level. Now that this necessity is absent and the labourers can afford a state of living as *petit bourgeois* the gainful employment of their wives reminds them of the period of poverty of the working-class at the time of their fathers and grandfathers. [3]

We have to realize that our society is involved in very rapid developments. The same prosperity that made female labour no longer necessary gave a stimulus to additional earnings of the married woman (part-time jobs, sometimes hidden for the authorities) in order to be able to participate in our society's extreme consumption, or in what is also called the affluent society. The middle-class layers of West European society went over from the pattern of female employment in the first years of marriage, to Szabady's third pattern and, with a time lag, the lower-income classes followed their example. For this reason it is difficult to say which pattern prevails within the West European countries. Individual preferences are important in this respect. Of course, the application of the yes-no-yes pattern number 3 within marriage also depends on the effective practice of birth control. Sometimes the idea is that the just-married woman is to hold her job for a number of years but a failure in birth-control shortens the period of her gainful employment. Important is also the spread of ideas about emancipation of the woman, connected with the pre-vailing mentality within different social circles. We may suggest here that the patriarchal family in Western Europe is most frequent among people belonging to the labour class. Another point is that Szabady's classification is based upon the identity of marriage and sexual union. So long as this identity is quite normal a classification of patterns concerning the employment of married women makes sense. As soon as the said identity is absent the official statistics are insufficient to discern patterns. I will come back to this point when dealing with my second example.

Szabady's first pattern is found in Eastern Europe. Two factors may pro-mote the coming into existence and maintenance of this pattern. One is the necessity of a national effort to raise the production. The other is the emancipa-tion of woman, rooted in ideology. Both factors might be important, as they are e.g. in Israel. The question may, of course, be raised whether this pattern will be stable for the next decades. The answer depends on the strength of the two factors here suggested. If there is no necessity of a national effort, will the countries here mentioned as examples maintain a high percentage of gain-fully employed married women for the age groups of over 25 or 30? Or will they take over the third pattern now found in the U.S.A., in France, in the U.K., but also, more incidentally, in other West European countries? A complete emancipation of woman, implying the right of self-determination regarding employment, might cause the shift in Western Europe to a pattern now already – or still – predominating in Eastern Europe. It is quite probable that women in Western Europe who now claim the right to be "mistress in own belly" (not only through birth control, but also abortion) will claim – and in fact do claim already – the right to be free as to their choice to take part in the labour, or not.

My second example, dealing with patterns of spacing births within mar-riage in Europe needs a rather long preamble. Several authors contributing to this volume give ample attention to marriage as an element in the change of numbers in aggregates. Now marriage is a juridical agreement, a contract with consequences for the contracting parties and for their possible offspring. This contract is not needed for the growth of a population, neither for a local or regional community nor for a religious group. We might say that marriage merely is a historical, social phenomenon and that it only as such is related to the growth of some aggregates. For the growth of numbers sexual unions are sufficient. In great parts of Latin America the official registered marriage is not a rule for all more or less stable sexual unions. Marriage in these areas, however, has a high status, as has an expensive wedding festivity. We all know too, that in Western Europe up to recently the unmarried mother was not much appreciated and sometimes near to being ostracized.

Of paramount importance in the history of Europe was that marriage was not primarily an affair of the State but of the church. For centuries the stable sexual unions have been registered by the church. It had the character of a sacrament. This meant that children were born within an institution surrounded by deeply rooted religious feelings. For this reason the institution of the formalized sexual union, called marriage, got a central place in European society. One might suggest that after the disestablishment of Church marriage might lose its sacred character and that marriage registered by the state might have less prestige. In those countries where marriage was secularized by the separation of state and church it nevertheless maintained a semi-sacred nature, no matter whether a clergyman consecrated the civil marriage afterward. In a country like the Netherlands an employee of the registrar's office, sometimes in a gown, in fact made the simple act of the registration of a formalized sexual union into an impressive ceremony. Marrying is still something very different from merely signing a contract or being registered by the state. In sociological terms we can say that there was a cultural lag of centuries.

Apart from the semi-sacred character of marriage in a period of growing secularization this institution and its juridical consequences secured the position of possible children and of their mother. So long as there were no effective means of birth-control there was an urgent need for such an institution. In our time, in which religion is losing its grip on society more and more, and the use of the contraceptive pill is widespread, the position of marriage is endangered, albeit only to a slight degree so far. The welfare state also made a contribution in this direction. War-widows might lose their pension in case they enter a second marriage or if a man and a woman of over 65 together get more old-age pension from the state in case they do not marry than in case they marry, why should they go to the registrar's to have their sexual union formalized? The last problem is actual now in old-age homes. And now that public opinion is far more liberal to what in fact is concubinage a formal marriage is not contracted.

For demographers formerly having marriage figures as part of reliable vital statistics this development creates some problems, especially when trying to construct patterns of the rhythm of reproduction within marriage. That old people do not marry is, of course, not very interesting, their contribution to the number of births being nil. As soon, however, as young people do not give notice of their sexual union officially young people are not always convinced of the "use" of legal marriage. It is cheaper to live together than seperately. But why marry? Perhaps it has a fiscal advantage not to do so, because with a system of progressive income taxes, two moderate incomes will be taxed less separately, than as their sum. It is true, however, that the increase in the number of de facto concubinages in many cases is not caused by fiscal factors. It is often simply the lack of a strong motive to marry that keeps the partners from having their union legally registered. Public opinion formerly exercising a strong social control on sexual unions, is rather permissive in several countries nowadays; religion has lost its hold on substantial parts of the population. Young people may decide themselves whether they prefer the legal union or the "alternative" one. Perhaps they stress the "experimental" character of their union, without legal implications, and therefore easily dissolvable, although of course a growing number of material properties held in common may be a serious obstacle for dissolution after some time. As a matter of fact, the increase of the number of alternative unions presupposes the effective and consistent use of the pill or of another reliable device. Pregnancy is still a strong motive to marry.

The problem for the demographer is that he has no exact figures as to the beginning of sexual unions and for this reason a classification of reproductive behaviour within marriage is rather arbitrary as an indication for this behaviour is related to stable sexual unions.

In the Dutch literature (see the contribution of H. G. Moors) nevertheless a classification of behavioural patterns has been proposed. I do not repeat this classification at full extent. I restrict myself to the most important types.

1. Traditional pattern. The couples do not practise any birth-control at all for moral, ethical or religious reasons. It is questionable of course whether this pattern is really wide spread. Very big families, however, still exist.
2. Rational pattern I. This pattern is characterized by a planned rapid creation of a family. In the first years of the marriage there is no birth-control. The interval between the marriage date and the first birth is short, as is the next interval between the first and the second child. The same holds true for third conception if any. As a rule the number of children is two or three. Within, let us say, five years the family has been completed and after completion effective birth-control will be practised.
3. Rational pattern II. Within the first years of the marriage the couple plans not to have children. The first child will be postponed by effective birth-control. As soon as the partners agree to raise a family they finish this off as quickly as possible. A family of two or three children therefore will be completed within 4 or 5 years. I may add here that the given figures (of number of children, of number of years of reproduction) are only indicative.

My first comment on this classification is that it runs parallel with the typology of female labour. If there is in principle no family planning, there is less reason to locate the labour of the married woman in a special period of the marriage. One may suppose that the mother is working in between the confinements or may not try to go into the labour market at all. Important variables will be income, legislation concerning allowances, child-care and so on, or the occupation of the husband (e.g. agriculture, or retail-trade). The first rational pattern corresponds to a pattern of no employment, followed later on by employment (no-yes), the second to a pattern of yes-no-yes. An analysis of the relation between the two typologies, however, has still to be made. If in Western Europe it would become normal for the married woman to take up a job after having finished procreation, the two rational patterns of family raising differ only as to the period the partners wish to have the children born, during which period the wife is not working outside home.

I now want to emphasize the fact that the uncertainty of where to fix the beginning of the stable sexual union has important implications for a classification of procreative behaviour during that union. It cannot be verified whether sexual unions, belonging formally to the first rational type because they have their limited number of children immediately after contracting the marriage, in fact do not belong to the second rational pattern, implying the postponement of confinements, if we take into account the years the unions already had existed as concubinages. An analysis of the relation between types of procreative behaviour and labour of married women is also difficult: what seem to be examples of the no-yes type (no employment followed by employment) taking as a starting-point only the formal one in fact belong to the yes-no-yes type, because during the period preceding the marriage the female partner had, sometimes for a rather long time, been gainfully employed. Official vital statistics cannot help us in solving this problem. Special surveys will be necessary. In case marriage will become less and less "popular" the reproductive behaviour of marriage-partners will be poly-interpretable so long as no additional data will be at hand from special sample surveys. Premarital intercourse has been quite normal throughout the history of mankind. The number of "enforced" marriages therefore speaks for itself. This type of marriage has so far offered only minor problems for demographic behaviour. In the classification by Moors it is included as a definite pattern because its procreative features are of a specific kind. Now that premarital intercourse in a situation of wide-spread knowledge of contraceptive methods in many cases does not lead quickly to marriage, the analysis of the behaviour of partners in stable sexual unions is hampered. A decrease of the marriage rate, as in Sweden over recent years (see the contribution of Trost; for the trends in other countries see the article by Wunsch), is now difficult to interpret.

IV. The reliability of demographic data

Definitions play an important role in demography. Szabady's exposition reminds us of the necessity to make a clear distinction between still birth and live birth. Another point of interest is to define who is a migrant. Formerly, the man or woman who changed permanent residence was a migrant. Statistically there is no problem, so long as statistics are reliable. But are they reliable in fact? Stefanow points out the phenomenon that restriction on migration to large cities in Bulgaria were got round through fictitious marriages or through granting temporary residence. People possessing a temporary permission to settle in a city live and work in a different place for years. They are not covered by the official statistics of migration. We as demographers, also know that one of the classical reasons to organize a census is to improve the registration of the population, especially as to the place of residence.

In our days the migrant has found his counterpart in the commuter. For numbers and changes in numbers of a local community migration is an essential factor. The commuter, however, who lives somewhere and is registered at that place, during day-time joins the working-population of another town, and his social and economic contribution to society is more essential for the place where he works than for where he has his domicile. For the description of social reality we are in bad need of good statistics of commuting. The distances people are willing to travel to work have been extended strikingly as an effect of better means of communication.

We may make the hypothesis that the official figures on residence and migration have suffered a great deal from the effects of state intervention. Stefanow's example already gave an indication. In a country like the Netherlands – and there is strong reason to suppose that the same sort of phenomena may be found in other countries of Europe – it may be advantageous to have a formal residence in one city and to live elsewhere in fact, because the norms of social assistance are more profitable. The Dutch tax system is such, that for a father whose son is a student it is lucrative to have him formally lodged elsewhere – in the same town or in another one, where the school has its residence – while the son in fact lives with his parents. In order to be registered on a waiting-list for a house it is better to be a resident of the community, renting a room somewhere, but in fact staying outside this community. Rules resulting from the housing shortage, e.g. that one may only be a candidate for a house if economically bound to a community, of course invite dodging. With the shortage of houses still prevailing in many countries several communities will have their clandestine residents.

I shall not come back to the difficulty of relying on the formal definition of marriage. In countries where divorce is very difficult to obtain or, as in Italy, up till recently practically impossible an analysis of wrecked marriages as a matter of fact is not an easy enterprise. What does it mean that the divorce-rate is going up? Does it really mean that there is less happiness in marriage? Or does it only reflect that the barriers against divorce – legal, traditional or religious ones – are becoming less strong than they were before? And if the number of concubinages increases (see above) is not a dissolution of such unions, if stable for, let us say, at least two years, sociologically speaking the same as a divorce? There are no legal drawbacks to the dissolutions of such unions. In cases where there is a formal marriage and therefore a legal barrier to dissolve the marriage contract, the refusal of one of the parties to consent to a divorce will lower the formal divorce-rate, although in sociological terms there is no marriage at all.

All over Europe the figures on birth and death are reliable. Lots of variables playing a part in demographic analysis, however, have to be critically scrutinized. Not only the variable of migration, marriage and divorce, but also a temporary element such as female labour, especially part-time labour. For several reasons female labour has always been underrated. There is the fiscal reason; the temporary character of female labour is relevant, too. Moreover, there is labour directly connected with houshold and family-life, as is the case with women's contribution to agriculture. As the importance of agriculture is rapidly decreasing in Western as well as in Eastern Europe, the last phenomenon is disappearing. Another figure reliable to a high extent is religious adherence. Now that the secularization process is wide-spread in Europe, the real strength in numbers of the different religious denominations is very difficult to define. In countries where the official figure of people not belonging to a denomination is rather low, this does not mean that all the others really belong to one of the churches or sects. Tradition still plays a part when people make known that they belong to a religious group, whilst in fact they have no relation at all to this group. This fact makes figures concerning the distribution of population according to denominations rather doubtful. Today in countries with a population mixed as to religion it is no longer easy to say who is a Roman-Catholic, who is a Lutheran, who is a Calvinist.

V. Summary

In my introduction I pointed out that demography, of course, has a core, but no limits. The contribution to this volume, especially if commented upon as I did in this comprehensive article, may sufficiently illustrated the point I made. Demographers, in fact, are roaming about the domains of several disciplines. The social and economic changes within Europe promote this dispersion. The industrialization of all countries, including those of Eastern Europe, the urbanization and suburbanization, the secularization process and the emancipation of woman, the rise of the welfare-state, the improvement of education, the changes of the labour-market, the ever lasting housing shortage and the expanding communication facilities, all these factors have aroused the interest of the demographer. A journal like the French Population has for a long time dealt all sorts of sociological and economic phenomena. Vital statistics, considered the backbone of demography, perhaps still are the starting-point for demographic studies; they have to be supplemented, however, by sample surveys and case studies. Demography is no more an activity to be carried out by scholars studying official statistics, sitting in their armchairs. The demographer has to gather his own data in addition to what a central bureau of statistics or a census bureau may offer him. The demographer nowadays is a fieldworker in society. He may be still interested in birth and death rates. But what matters to him more are motivations and effects. He needs an insight into shifts in religious convictions, into the housing problem, into the position of the institution of marriage in society. He deals with the consequences of the old-age problem and of changes in the educational system. His activity in the present situation is interdisciplinary, in the real sense of the word. He is unable to say whether he is an economist, a psychologist or a sociologist. He is not able to indicate precisely what he is doing, or in which part of reality he is working. He will simply feel a demographer, and he will trust that others will be satisfied with this answer. He justifies his activities by the results of his work.

BIBLIOGRAPHY

[1] E. G. Ravenstein, On the laws of migration, *Journal of the Statistical society*, 1885, p. 168–174, 1889, p. 274–275.

[2] J. Hajnal, European marriage patterns in perspective, D. V. Glass and D. C. Eversley; *Population in history*, London, 1965, p. 101–143.

     J. Matras, The social strategy of family formation: some variations in time and space, *Demography 2*, 1965, p. 349–362.

     N. Ryder, The character of modern fertility, *The Annals*, 1967, p. 26–36.

     E. W. Hofstee, De groei van de Nederlandse bevolking (The growth of the Dutch population), *Drift en Koers*, Assen, 1962, p. 27–28.

[3] H. Verwey-Jonker, Speech delivered at a symposion in The Hague on 12 May 1971, *Randstad Data*, 1971/2.

The Social and Demographic Changes of Hungarian Society during the last 25 Years[1]

EGON SZABADY

Budapest

I

THE fundamental features of the social transformation which took place in Hungary are generally known. Public opinion is, however, less informed about the dimension of the changes in the structure of society and about the trends and character of the processes which brought about these changes.

The exact description of the social changes and, in addition to this, the analysis of the interrelations demand empirical, documentary information on the one hand, and the exploration of the connections between the factors instrumental in the change in question, on the other. The complexity of the factors in this regard is generally known: economic, social, political, technical cultural, demographic and sanitary elements can equally have a role – both separately and in interrelation with one another – in the formation of society. To disregard any of the groups of factors involves the risk of simplification and, through this, of distorting reality.

At the same time, for practical reasons the trends and aspects of the examinations and analyses are, of necessity, limited. Admitting, and even, emphasizing the necessity of an interdisciplinary attitude, the present study intends, therefore, to approach the question from the angle of demography, relying in the first place on statistical data. An approach of this kind is justified on the one hand by the recognition that in social sciences the empirical and quantitative attitude cannot be dispensed with. On the other hand, owing to the interdisciplinary character of demography, the demographical outlook somewhat diminishes the danger of one-sidedness.

Nevertheless, both the character of the data at disposal and the extent of this study call for setting out the bounds of the theme and the structure of its discussion. Founded on the logical order of the analysis – also considering the points resulting from the character of the material at disposal – the development of the following outline seems expedient:

---

1 Statisztikai Szemle (Statistical Review), Vol. 48, No. 4.

I. The modification of the social structure in connection with the structural changes of national economy.

II. The processes giving rise to the structural changes; intergeneration-, intrageneration- and marriage mobility.

III. The role of the cultural factors (educational level) in social mobility.

IV. The change in the socio-economic role of women: its effect on the structure of micro-society (the family) and macrosociety (the population).

V. The social causes and consequences of the demographic changes (age-structure, aging, family status, fall in birth-rate).

II

It was the rapid progress and transformation of the national economy, which exerted the greatest influence on the structure of Hungarian society in the past 25 years. As a consequence of these, a marked change took place

a) in the number and rate of the earners,
b) in their distribution by branches of national economy,
c) in their distribution by the character of the posts held by them.

a) As a consequence of the considerable increase of the rate of employment in the period of industrialization, *the number of earners* grew from the 4,4 millions of the year 1944, to 5.9 millions by 1968 (see Table 1). *Their rate* within the total population was, against the 48 per cent value of the year 1949, as much as 58 per cent in 1968[2]. This favourable development of rates as regards living standards and income level (109 dependants fell to 100 earners in 1949, whereas in 1969 this rate was only 74) is counteracted to some extent by the circumstance that the increase of the number of inactive earners (pensioners) was the most rapid among the earners: their number grew to more than its fourfold, their rate rose from 3 to 11 per cent of the total population. In consequence of this, the index expressing the measure of economic productivity, the ratio of dependants and inactive earners falling to 100 earners, decreased from the value 122 of the year 1949 to but 114 by 1968; consequently, the measure of the decrease was much smaller than indicated by the ratio earners-dependants, relevant in respect of the distribution of income. In view of the further trends to be expected in this regard – to the discussion of which the author shall revert in section VI –, the considerable socio-economic significance of the difference between the two indices should be especially stressed.

---

2 Although the present study examines changes which took place in the course of 25 years, from practical reasons it often has no choice but to consider the period 1949–1968, regarding which there are appropriate data at disposal. However, since the time between 1945 and 1949 was in many respects – in those of economy and demography alike – the period of reconstruction, of returning to the pre-war situation, the data yielded by the 1949 and 1941 population censuses are, in seceral relations, similar.

Table 1

Trend of the number of earners and dependants

Specification	Number (thousand persons) of population				Distribution (per cent) of population			
	1949	1960	1963	1968	1949	1960	1963	1968
Active earners	4,154	4,760	4,649	4,791	45	48	46	47
Inactive earners	255	436	774	1,106	3	4	8	11
Dependants	4,796	4,765	4,649	4,339	52	48	46	42
Population total	9,205	9,961	10,072	10,236	100	100	100	100

The increase in number and proportion of the earners was, besides the primarily economic factors, also connected with certain demographic phenomena (e.g. with the change of age-structure). However, it was the increasing employment of women, which had the most important part in this respect. As mentioned above, the author will deal with the socio-economic aspects of this separately.

b) The greatest changes in the composition of Hungarian society were brought about by the modification of the structure of national economy. The formerly dominant proportion of agriculture, which had hardly changed since the turn of the century, rapidly decreased after 1949. The number of persons employed in agriculture decreased by nearly 1 million (from 2.2 millions to

Table 2

Composition of the active earning population by branches of national economy

Date	Number of active earners	Of these				
		Agriculture	Industry, building industry	Communication	Commerce	Other branches of national economy
	Numerically (thousand persons)					
January 1st, 1949	4,154	2,196	963	165	220	610
January 1st, 1968	4,791	1,286	2,017	321	361	806
	Percentage					
January 1st, 1949	100.0	52.8	23.2	4.0	5.3	14.7
January 1st, 1968	100.0	26.9	42.1	6.7	7.5	16.8

1.3 million), their rate among all earners fell from a value exceeding 50 per cent to a one below 30 per cent. At the same time a development of contrary direction ensued in industry, building industry and communication: the number of employees increased from 1.1 million to 2.3 millions. Especially in the last 10 years, a significant increase also presented itself in the other, non-agricultural branches of national economy (commerce, services).

The data of distribution by type of engagement, most important in social respect, reflect the above changes. While in 1949 the number of the independent and unpaid family workers was still dominant, in our days the overwhelming majority of the earners consist of the strata of workers and employees, as well as of the members of co-operatives.

Table 3

Distribution of active earners by character of employment

Character of employment	Number of active earners (per cent)			
	1949	1960	1963	1968
Employees	46	63	69	76
Members of cooperatives	—	15	27	20
Independents and unpaid family workers	54	22	4	4
Total	100	100	100	100

The social effects of the change in the economic structure, manifested in the modification of the occupational composition of the population, are manifold and far-reaching. Merely as an example, the author can refer here to the acceleration of the process of urbanization. A manifestation of this: the rate of urban population, having displayed a slow but steady increase from 37 per cent of the year 1949, reached 44 per cent in 1968. On the other hand, some urbanization phenomena (electricity supply, public utilities, sanitary and cultural institutions), greatly preas in settlements also, which, in respect of public administration, are qualified as villages.

c) During the examined period a radical change took place in the individual distribution by the occupation of the earners, in that by the *character of their posts held*. Partly as a consequence of the technical improvement, partly of the formation of greater economic-organizational units, the number of the posts demanding higher skill rapidly increased. On the other hand, a general and intense preference was shown for the lighter kind of office-work within the population, especially among women and younger age-groups, which, in many places, increased the number of the non-physical workers in a measure exceeding the objectieve demands. As a joint effect of these two factors, the proportion of physical and intellectual workers, which could be estimated 87–13 per cent at the end of the 1940's, changed to 76–24 per cent by 1968. A detailed investigation into the question of how far this shifting of the proportions was justified and necessary, goes beyond the compass of this study. Undoubtedly, this trend is generally to be observed in the highly developed countries and is, to a certain measure, concomitant with up-to-date technology and organization. However, the extraordinary pace and measure of the shift in proportion in Hungary give rise to reflection. It is just possible that orientation motivated by prestige, which is generally to be observed in the choice of profession and by far not favourable for economic productivity, could lead to the formation of unfounded proportions in certain fields.

This can be judged, of course, only when founding oneself on concrete studies, on examining the possibilities of technology and plant organization. The national data-the ratio of 3 to 1 of the physical and intellectual workers-direct attention to the actuality of the question at any rate.

On account of its significance, a detailed examination of the change which took place in the occupational data in the past 8 years seems reasonable. The number of physical workers has continuously decreased since 1960: by 8 per cent in 8 years.

Table 4

Branch of national economy	Number (thousand persons) of manual workers			Distribution (per cent)			In the year 1968 expressed in per cent of the 1960 values
	1960	1963	1968	1960	1963	1968	
Agriculture	1,710	1,307	944	43	35	26	55
Industry	940	1,013	1,180	24	27	32	126
Building and construction	216	221	275	5	6	7	127
Commerce	155	160	183	4	4	5	118
Communication and telecommunication	207	242	277	5	7	8	134
Services and others	736	804	796	19	21	22	108
Together	3,964	3,747	3,655	100	100	100	92

This was called forth by the rapid regress of the number of the manual workers of agriculture (from 1.7 million to 0.9 million); in the other branches of the national economy the number of the manual workers showed an increase. As a result of the changes, in 1968 the occupation of nearly a third of the 3.655,000 manual workers was industrial, that of slightly more than a quarter of this number was of agricultural character.

The regress of the number of the population active in agriculture is of even greater measure than appears from the data given above. This is connected with the recent practice, according to which the farms, partly in the interest of a proper employment of labour power and partly to increase profit, also undertake industrial activities etc. beside agricultural work. Partly by this it can be explained that, while only 7 per cent of the manual workers employed in agriculture had been of non-agricultural occupation in 1960, communication, etc. activities in 1968.

Among those of industrial occupation, the number of fitters, metal-turners, motor-vehicle and engine mechanics, technicians and welders increased significantly during the last 8 years.

Table 5

Trends of some selected individual occupations in industry

	Number of persons of industrial occupation (thousand persons)			In the year 1968 expressed in per cent of the 1960 values
	1960	*1963*	*1968*	
Locksmith	107	118	155	145
Tailor, cutter, dressmaker	63	64	87	138
Metal-turner	30	37	51	170
Motor-vehical and engine mechanic	20	25	49	245
Miner	45	51	47	104
Joiner	39	41	46	118
Mechanician	24	28	45	188
Welder and other occupation in the metal industry	31	38	44	142
Weaver	36	38	43	119
Shoemaker and other occupation in the shoeindustry	37	35	34	92

The number of persons of intellectual occupation has increased by 340,000 (43 per cent) since 1960.

The rise amounted to more than 150,000 with the office workers, to more than 100,000 with the technical directing staff and skilled workers, to 75,000 with scientific, cultural and sanitary workers. As it emerges from these changes, nearly half (44 per cent) of the intellectual workers continued to be office workers, and 25 per cent each belonged to the groups of technical and/or scientific, cultural and sanitary workers.

III

In the preceding section of this study, the differences presenting themselves in the composition of society at the beginning and end of the examined period were outlined. In several countries this is the sole examination method at disposal: a comparison of the data of different dates and to draw conclusions there

Table 6

Distribution of non-manual workers according to posts held

Occupational group	Number (thousand persons)			Distribution (per cent)			In the year 1968 expressed in per cent of 1960 values
	1960	1963	1968	1960	1963	1968	
Engineers in responsible positions	80	89	111	10	10	9	139
Senior officials in charge of science, culture and public health	103	110	146	13	12	13	142
Administrative and economic executives	54	59	66	7	7	6	122
Senior officials and executives together	237	258	323	30	29	28	136
Technical staff workers	106	124	176	13	14	16	166
Scientific, cultural and sanitary staff workers	105	112	137	13	12	12	130
Staff workers together	211	236	313	26	26	28	148
Office workers	348	408	500	44	45	44	144
Total	796	902	1,136	100	100	100	143

from regarding the processes which took place in the meantime. Evidently, however, when conducting thorough research, one cannot content oneself with that only. In the respect of society, namely, not only the final results are of basic importance, but also the trend and intensity of the processes causing them. Identical endresults may ensue as consequences of social processes of entirely different character and proportion. This can also be illustrated by a numerical example. If a group of 100 persons is distributed in a ratio of 50 to 50 at the beginning of the examined period and in a ratio of 60 to 40 at the end, then this can happen in the following ways:

a) 10 persons have gone over from the first group to the second one, but also that

b) 30 persons have gone over from the first to the second and, at the same time, 20 from the second to the first group.

Evidently, in spite of the identical results, the problems of the two situations differ significantly. This was the circumstance which directed the author's research to the examination of the processes of social regrouping, of mobility.

With the basic types of social mobility in mind, three main types of mobility can be distinguished:

A) intrageneration mobility: change of the social position, layer, occupation during the given person's lifetime;

B) intergeneration mobility: change of the social position as compared with the status of the father;

C) marriage mobility: change of the social stratum in connection with marriage.

A) Without intending to enlarge upon the pertinent questions of methodology in this study, it should be mentioned that the examination of intrageneration mobility can be done in two ways. Either it is examined, whether those persons within a given present social stratum, did previously change their position or not (accession mobility), or the proportion is sought for in which the persons occupying an originally defined social position, have modified the same (secession mobility). This distinction is most essential as regards just the present examination, since, as this will be shown below, the results of the examinations conducted in Hungary of these two aspects present rather differing pictures.

Examining accession mobility, i.e. setting out from the present situation, one can state that it is the last one of the three fundamental strata (non-agricultural manual workers, agricultural manuel workers and non-manual workers) which presents the most intense mobility. For instance, in Budapest but 46 per cent of the present non-manual workers always belonged to this group; further, 35 per cent had changed into non-manual from non-agricultural manual workers, and 4 per cent had been agricultural manual workers before. In addition, 15 per cent of the present: non-manual workers were originally similarly non-manual, but had followed also manual professions in the course of their lives.

As to accession, the layer of the non-agricultural manual workers takes in an intermediary position regarding mobility. 71 per cent of these always belonged to this stratum, 16 per cent came from among the manual workers of agriculture and 6 per cent from the non-manual workers. Finally, 7 per cent is the rate of those manual workers who had originally been manual workers of agriculture, subsequently non-manual workers, and came from there among the non-agricultural manual workers.

Results similar to the 1963 Budapest data outlined above are also presented by the examination conducted simultaneously in cities of the country. From these it appears, further, that as to accession, the least mobile of the strata is that of the manual workers of agriculture. This is also supported by the pertinent examinations carried out in villages. According to these more than 90 per cent of the present-day agricultural manual workers also originally belonged to this social layer.

Quite a different picture is presented, if one examines the question from another angle: from that of the secessions. In other words: if one seeks for the proportion in which the persons belonging to the social strata are changing their occupation to an extent which means going over to another social stratum.

According to the examinations of the year 1963 in Budapest and in the cities of the country, the rates of secession range around 10–14 per cent with non-manual workers. Consequently, the overwhelming majority of those who had started their career as non-manual workers, permanently remained in that category. Only every eighth or tenth among the non-manual became a manual worker.

With the non-agricultural manual workers the rate of secession is higher: 22–25 per cent. The majority of the seceding population goes over to the category of the non-manual workers, and only an insignificant part enters the group of the manual workers of agriculture.

Lastly, the rate of secession is the highest (25–30 per cent) with the stratum of the manual workers of agriculture, the majority of whom become non-agricultural manual workers.

Thus, summing up the above, there were two main trends to be observed in intrageneration mobility:

the regrouping of persons of agricultural occupation into the category of non-agricultural manual workers,
and the mobilization of the manual workers among those of non-manual occupation.

In consequence of all this, it was the stratum of the non-manual workers which has become the most heterogeneous as regards origin; mainly the non-agricultural manual workers went over to this social layer. As to heterogenity, the stratum of the non-agricultural manual workers has an intermediate position (with an intense outflow toward the non-manual workers and an inflow from among the manual workers of agriculture) and, finally, the stratum of the manual workers is the most closed one; hardly any inflow into this stratum from others takes place.

The character of mobility within one generation was thus, in connection with industralization and the increasing proportion of non-manual occupations, almost unambiguously upward. Declassation occured in but relatively insignificant proportion: the intense mobilization toward the intelligentsia on the part of the manual strata did not mean that the strata making debut as non-manual workers were cousted from their original occupation, although undoubtedly also the sign of this could be noticed sporadically and in certain periods: to this refers also the fact, that, that some 15–20 per cent of those active, both originally and at present, in a non-manual profession, temporarily pursued a manual occupation in the meantime. Social regrouping and the trend toward the non-manual and non-agricultural manual occupations was thus rendered possible and necessary by the transformation of national economy.

B) The picture presented by the examination of the *regrouping between generations* is similar in its character, but, of course, different in its proportions. Examining the proportions of secession, also here the persons of agricultural occupation rank first: among 100 fathers of agricultural occupation the sons of but 41 are to be found in the same social stratum, 50 have gone over to the non-agricultural manual stratum and 9 to that of the non-manual workers. With the non-agricultural manual workers the rate of remaining in the original stratum is 70 per cent, that if those having gone over among the non-manual workers is 24 per cent, of those gone over to manual workers of agriculture is 6 per cent. With non-manual workers the rate of remaining in the stratum is 68 per cent, that of going over among non-agricultural manual workers is 30, that of going over to agriculture is 2 per cent. Hence intergeneration mobility is greater as to its dimensions, and – although, regarding its character, it is determined similarly by the process of urbanization in a decisive measure – is not quite so unambiguous in its direction as this was seen above with intra-generation mobility. So for instance, in the case of the non-manual workers; the proportion of those whose children go over to the stratum of manual workers, amounts to nearly two thirds. However, it should be mentioned that compared with the relevant data of the developed countries, this proportion cannot be considered high at all; the data at disposal about the United States, Sweden, the German Federal Republic or France present similar proportions.

As a result of the intergeneration processes outlined above, the structure as regards origin of the non-manual workers is the most heterogeneous one of all: only 29 per cent of them descended from parents who were non-manual workers, 45 per cent from non-agricultural manual workers and 26 per cent from agricultural physical workers. The parents of 44 per cent of the non-agricultural manual workers belonged to the same category, those of 52 per cent were agricultural manual workers and 4 per cent of them came from the stratum of the non-manual workers. In this respect, similarly, the stratum of the agricultural workers is the most closed one; with these the proportion of homogeneity is 90 per cent.

C) Besides occupational mobility, also the data referring to marriage mobility demonstrate the open and/or closed character and communication between the social strata.

The choice of the partner in marriage is an individual move of behaviour, founded on personal decision. However, in the trends manifested in the statistical data also the social judgement is reflected, which has been formed by the members of the social stratum about themselves, about other strata and about the relation of their own group and those. From the data of the Hungarian marriage statistics it can be concluded that the consciousness of belonging to a social stratum is still a significant psychological motivating factor in this country. In more than two thirds of the marriages, the husband and the wife belonged to identical social strata. The association indexes show that, with the non-manual and agricultural strata, the frequency of homogeneous marriages is the 2–3 fold of the value it would reach in case of even distribution or of a choise of mates regardless to social prejudices. The group of the non-agricultural manual workers is relatively the most open one as to matrimonial mobility, although even here certain preference can be observed. Among the marriages between heterogeneous persons, i.e. who belong to different social strata, those between non-agricultural manual and non-manual workers are the most frequent ones. Within these the marriages where the husband is a manual, the wife a non-manual worker, outnumber the others; however also the opposite is relatively frequent, which is indicative of a diminution of the differences between the two strata in this regard. To another major group of heretogeneous marriages belong those between persons from the layers of non-agricultural and agricultural manual workers. However, in the overwhelming majority of the cases of this category it is the man who belongs to the group of non-agricultural manual and the woman to that of the agricultural manual workers, which is evidently connected with the higher occupational mobility of the men.

The marriages between persons from the non-manual and the agricultural-manual layers are relatively infrequent, which indicates that these two occupational groups are farthest from each other in the public opinion.

Summarizing the examinations concerning social mobility, it can be stated that following the large-scale regrouping in mostly upward direction, necessitated by economic development and made possible by the cultural revolution, the open character of Hungarian society has become more intense, and the mobility between the strata has increased. Nevertheless the differences between the social strata, presented in the character of work and in income-level, still make their effects felt among the population, and, for instance, preference is manifested by marriages within the same social stratum. Mobility and contact between the strata are the most intense on the one part in the non-agricultural manual – non-manual relation and in the non-manual – agricultural-manual one on the other; the non-manual and agricultural-manual strata are still far enough from one another, and rather markedly separated. Still additional phases of technical and social progress are needed for a further increase of the open character of Hungarian society in this regard.

IV

One of the most essential changes in the life of Hungarian society was brought about by the *development of cultural relations*. This has manifested itself basically in two directions. Partly in the general rise of the educational level, partly in the increase of the demands on and in the change of the forms of education, connected primarily with the general use of the means of mass communication.

The factor mentioned second has a part mainly in the modification of the way in which people spend their leisure-time, According to examinations conducted in this regard, listening to the radio and watching television is dominating in leisure-time to a continuously greater extent and, within this, especially in the time spent for education. Theatre and reading have been somewhat eclipsed; moreover, following the general spread of television even cinema has lost part of its attendance. During the past 25 years the use of means of mass communication (radio, television, motion pictures, press) has reached mass-dimensions and become general both in the country and in the cities. These means opened the way for culturally approaching even such social strata which were deprived of any possibility of education or more civilized entertainment facilities before. The group which does not at all avail itself of the said means can be estimated at only 4 per cent of the population at present.

The social significance of the means of mass communication is illustrated by the fact that they take up about 90 per cent of the time spent on education. On the other hand, this somewhat one-sided proportion indicates that although our society has made the best use of the new possibilities afforded by technology in a short time, and created by this new and significant demands in a certain direction, it has not yet informed its expectations toward each of the cultural branches, and is, for this reason, not yet able to develop sound proportions of the various branches of education. In the author's opinion, Hungarian cultural life should take notice of this phenomenon, lest the mechanized, passive forms of education should overshadow e.g. reading, which is an essential condition of a higher, well-established cultural level.

While the expansion and structural change of the forms of education rather affected the utilization of free time, the rise of the level of schooling was also in direct connection with the occupational-social regrouping of the population. The intense upward mobility, discussed in the previous section of this study was made possible, in the first place, by the vast spread of instruction. It should be noted that, contrary to the majority of socio-demographic processes, which began at the end of the 1940s (as this has been referred to above), in this regard an essential advance had taken place as early as immediately after the liberation of the country. As a result of this, the rate of those within the 15 years' old population who had finished the course of the 8th grade of public elementary school increased from 15 per cent in the year 1941 to as much as 21 per cent by 1968. The education and instruction of the groups of schooling-age can be considered practically complete. From the population of the ages concerned, the 1941 percentage of those having taken their final examination from secondary school increased to 6 per cent by 1949 and to 15 per cent by 1968. At the same time the proportion of university and college graduates increased from 2 to 4 per cent.

Besides the rise of the general level of instruction, in higher education also the structure of training was modified in accordance with the economic demands, and a certain specialization also began in secondary education.

During the first part of the period under examination, harmony between the trend and structure of instruction and professional training and the demands of economy was, in general, ensured – apart from minor discrepancies – by the considerable absorbing capacity of national economy. Demand for higher and even middle-grade specialists was so great that employers practically queued up at the institutes of education for engaging school-leavers and graduating students. This situation has gradually changed in the last 10–12 years. Although in several professional fields lack of specialists is still to be observed, in others saturation already entails certain difficulties in finding employment for those who have finished school and in ensuring for them a suitable field of

Table 7

Rates of school attendance

	Of the		
	15	*18*	*25*
Year	*years old or older population*		
	have at least		*graduated from an institution of higher education*
	finished 8 years of el- ementary school	*taken final ex- amination at sec- ondary school*	
	Numerically (thousand persons)		
1941	1,039	266	85
1949	1,435	356	91
1960	2,439	615	163
1963	2,901	714	178
1968	3,878	1,094	251
1968 expressed in per cent of the 1963 values	134	153	141
	In per cent of the population of respective age		
1941	15	4	2
1949	21	6	2
1960	33	9	3
1963	38	10	3
1968	49	15	4

work. For instance, according to an examination conducted in 1963, in certain professions 10–12 per cent of the persons graduated from institutions of higher education had the feeling that they did not need their diploma for performing the duties concomitant with their places of work. Similar phenomena are also found among one part of the workers having a secondary and/or vocational-training qualification. After all, in the period under examination about 20,000 graduated and 280,000 skilled persons (having participated in the instruction of industrial apprentices) did not work where, according to their own judgement, they could make full use of their qualifications.

In the light of these processes, as well as in that of the questions also frequently discussed in radio and television programmes, it becomes more and more evident that a much finer and more detailed co-ordination of the conceptions of educational and economic policy is becoming more and more necessary to be able to keep the economic efficiency of education at an adequate level. The author should like to refer here to the circumstance that in nearly all developed countries the problem of economic efficiency of education is presenting itself. These countries have, namely, surpassed the level up to which the extension of education in any direction proved economical and efficient. The economic weight of the problem is increased by the considerable costs of special training, which continuously grow with the standard of qualification and the advance of technology. Consequently, economically unexploited qualification is to be considered a partly or totally useless investment of a considerable order of magnitude.

Also the aspects of social psychology of this theme deserve to be specially mentioned. The persons who have the feeling that they cannot, or can but inadequately use their qualification in their field of activity, feel disappointed, and think that their efforts expended to obtain their qualifications were vain. Thus, besides reasons of economic character, also social political interests are tied up with the necessity to restrict the number of such persons to a minimal level.

V

In the processes outlined above (modification of the occupational structure, regrouping, rise of the educational level) the marked *change in the socio-economic field brought about by activity of women* had an important part.

The rise of the employment rate, discussed in the foregoing, was brought about in the first place by the circumstance that women got employed in an increasing measure. The rate of employment of the men, or rather the demand for this among the adults (the 20–60 years old) came near to 100 per cent at any time; thus here the change was consisted partly of the liquidation of unemployment, partly of employing certain numerically small strata who had lived of unearned income before. At the same time the change ensued in the rate of female employment was rather significant. While round one third of the female population of respective age were earners in 1949, this proportion has risen to nearly two thirds in our days. Consequently, the rate of women in the earning population has grown from 30 per cent to nearly 40 per cent. In demographic respect it is worth attention that while the majority of earning women were unmarried, widows or divorced between the two World Wars, today, as a consequence of the fact that it has become general among married women and/or those who have a family to be employed, the majority of the women earners is married.

The combination of two functions (family, reproductive and socio-economic) of the women doubtlessly carries in the possibility of certain conflicts. According to the form in which the majority of women solve the contradiction of their double field of activity in the given situation, three types of female employment have developed in the highly industrialized countries.

Type I. Within the first type come those countries where the rate of the women earners between 20–55 years of age reaches approximately the same height (60–70 per cent). Among such countries belong for instance Bulgaria, Poland and Rumania.

Table 8

Rates of economic activity by sex and age

Active earners expressed in the percentage of the population of respective age

Age-group (years old)	men				women				together			
	1949	1960	1963	1968	1949	1960	1963	1968	1949	1960	1963	1968
20–29	95	97	95	94	39	52	57	68	66	74	76	81
20–39	98	99	99	99	30	50	55	63	62	73	76	80
40–59 years old men / 40–54 years old women	95	97	96	94	27	49	50	55	62	75	75	76

Type II. With the second group those countries can be ranked, where most of the woman earners are in their early 20s, subsequently their rate falls and remains at a low level to the end (for instance Belgium, the Netherlands, Italy, Sweden).

Type III. Within the third type fall those countries, where following the peak of employment in youth, the rate of the woman earners shows a temporary decrease but later however, toward the end of the 30s, it begins to increase and reaches another peak after the 40th year of life. A situation of this kind is to be observed in the United States, England and France.

The types specified above cover the women's different attitudes following childbirth and concerning the education of their children. The majority of the women belonging to the first type return to the place of their employment shortly after confinement. The majority of the women of the second type definitely give up their earning occupation if they have children. Finally, the women who fall under the third category, stay at home only until they deem necessary for the education of their children at home, and take up an earning occupation again when the children have reached a certain age (mostly schooling age).

The economic activity of the Hungarian female population cannot be unequivocally included in either of the above groups. At the end of the 1940s it most of all resembled the second type, the rate of the employed was high in the young age-groups, in the older ones it was lower. This, however, was a situation of rather transitory character, arising in the first place from the circumstance that with the older female population the motives to get employed did not appear in the same proportion as with the women of younger ages. Toward the end of the 1950s, an approach toward the first type seemed to take place, where the rate of employment is fairly high in all age-groups. Recently, mainly in connection with the introduction of child-care allowance and other benefits of a labouract, the signs of an approach to the third type are to be noticed, too.

Besides the labour-act's financial and population-political effects, the institution of child-care allowance, introduced in 1967[3], also has serious social political significance. More than two thirds of the women entitled did take advantage of the allowance, and the number of the mothers attending to their child under ten at home, is to be expected to settle between 130–140 thousand. This means 8 per cent of the earning female population; among the 20–29 years old this proportion can amount even to 20–25 per cent.

Concerning the views on child-care allowance – prior to its introduction and also since then – there have been vivid debates. On the one hand it is not to be questioned that the institution has a favourable effect on infants' and children's sanitation. In the infants' nurseries – where, for that matter, only

---

3   The system of child-care allowance ensures for the earner-mother the possibility to take unpaid holidays at her job when her maternity leave is finished – if she so decides – till her child has reached 3 years of age. During that period she is assisted by an allowance amounting to 30–40 per cent of her salary on the average.

10–12 per cent of the children below 3 years of age can be accommodated – the morbidity rate of the children, especially as regards infectious diseases and common colds, is significantly higher than among those kept at home. Consequently, taking care at home of children below 3 is by all means more favourable. On the other hand, misgivings arose as to whether childcare allowance would not withdraw women workers trained at considerable costs from economic life. The data obtained so far did not support these worries. Resorting to the allowance is inversely proportional to qualification, consequently the withdrawing effect of this benefit appears primarily in the fields of work where a lower qualification is required. Theoretically, it is in these routine-like, mechanical fields of work where temporary substitution can be realized with the least difficulty. However, undoubtedly the labour shortage, anyhow occurring in unpopular, relatively underpaid fields of work not receiving due social appreciation, may increase, if the female population is to receive child-care allowance. Also this should be borne in mind when framing the wages policy.

Opinions as differed as to how far the institution of the allowance was in harmony with the practical realization of the principle of equal rights for women, whether it did not hinder the extrafamiliair activity of women. In the author's opinion, however, the safeguarding of the possibility to choose does in no way mean as if the career of women were rendered more difficult. Without doubt, the temporary absence from economic activity can bring about a certain lag in the career of women; however, in the occupations where the rate of those availing themselves of the allowance is significant, this is, as a rule, not of major importance. For this reason the development of the so-called double-peak employment of women cannot be considered an unfavourable phenomenon, although it remains certain that the interrupted earning activity involves special labour, labour-psychological, trade, training, and other problems regarding both the women concerned and their place of work. Still, all these problems can be solved, and are eclipsed by the favourable social and demographic effects ensured by the allowance system. The author specially stresses the significance of the fact that with its cost of yearly 1 thousand million, child-care allowance has most effectively promoted the trend of births, which was hardly influenced e.g. when the system of family allowances was extended at much higher costs. In connection with the economic respects also the circumstance should be mentioned that in a crèche the monthly state donation by costs of accommodation for one infant amounts to about 1,000 Forints, i.e. it surpasses the sum of the child-care allowance to a significant measure. On the other hand, as a consequence of the laborious nature of the accommodation in nursery homes, the number of women employed in these institutions comes close to half of that of the substituted mothers.

The employment of women has greatly contributed to the shift that has taken place in the rates of manual and non-manual work outlined above. Female labour has showed, namely, a marked preference for non-manual professions and within this in the first place for administrative and office work, further for cultural and sanitary professions. As a consequence, women constitute only one third of the category of manual workers, they outnumber the men among the non-manual workers, their proportion among office workers is 70 per cent, and more than 60 per cent of those employed in the cultural and sanitary sectors. Apart from the traditionally female positions (for instance kindergarten teachers, stenographers and typists, nurses), in the administrative posts as well as in school-teaching their rate is continually increasing (70–80 per cent). The rate of women is rising, further in those non-manual professions (engineer, jurist, physician) where their training on a larger scale began only following the liberation.

The employment of women was greatly furthered – especially as regards non-manual positions – by the rapid rise in their educational levels and qualifications.

Table 9

Rates of school attendance by sex

Sex	Rate/per cent/of those		
	finished at least 8 years of elementary school	taken at least final examination at secondary school	graduated from an institution of higher education
	among the		
	15	18	25
	years old or older population		
	In 1949		
Men	22	8	3
Women	20	3	1
	In 1960		
Men	35	12	5
Women	31	6	1
	In 1963		
Men	41	13	5
Women	36	8	1
	In 1968		
Men	52	17	6
Women	45	12	2

Though there are still significant differences to be observed in school qualification to the advantage of the male population, this can practically be attributed to peculiarities of the educational system in force 25–30 years ago regards education, women are not infrequently in a much more advantageous position nowadays. The rate of girls among secondary-school students is 58 per cent. With academy and university students this rate is 45 per cent, which follows, however, solely from the rather low proportion of women students in the technical and agricultural branches of education (10–25 per cent). In all the other branches of study (pharmacist, teacher, economist, jurist) women outnumber the men. In view of the fact that the majority of those not making use of their qualification consists of women (the rate of the non-working women in active age, possessing diplomas from universities or academies is more than fivefold the similar proportion among men), the author deems these rates worth considering. In his opinion it should be examined, whether the process of feminization distinctly manifested in certain professions even today would not lead to adverse conditions in a certain part of the non-manual posts, if they spread wider.

The gainful employment of women at productive age had its effects not only on the structure of macro-society on the composition of the workers-, it also affected the size and division of work within the smallest social unit- the family and household. This effect was manifold. The type of peasants' and urban craftsmen's households, founded on a living together of the traditional three-generation joint families is, in general, being disorganized by industrialization, by large-scale production conditions, and these processes and conditions give rise to the formation of joint families consisting of two generations. At the same time, the earning occupation of the women at productive age – together with housing shortage – exerts a delaying effect on the said process. The importance of the grandparents in the provision for and education of small children is well-known: in case of common life and house-keeping, the performance of this function becomes easier, practically automatic.

As a resultant of all these effects, the average size of the families has continuously decreased. 3.26 persons fell to one family in 1960; in 1968 this value was only 3.18. Also the average size of families decreased to some degree, in spite of the fact that for instance the number of the 2-family households showed an increase between 1960 and 1968.

One of the demands inseparable from the employment of women was that of reducing housework, which in part meant a shifting of such activities to production and/or service. An interesting – as yet unperformed – task of research could be to ascertain the order of the function of this process e.g. in the development of the food industry or public services. However, it is evident even without factual data that the rate of the mechanized households, using kitchen-ready food is continuously increasing, and, what is natural, in the first place with the families where also the woman is in employment. This shift of housework to be observed in each technically developed society, has its effect on the trend of housing culture and of the formation of the life at home of the families, in general.

VI

Besides the transformation caused by economic and political factors, also changes brought about by demographic factors have ensued in the course of the past 25 years. Just for lack of being directly related with policy, these changes are not being duly observed at all times, although, owing to their character and effects they are of extraordinary significance.

One of these changes is the modification of the population's age-structure. As regards its age-structure, Hungarian population is much older today than ever in the course of history. This was caused partly by the lengthening of the average duration of life called forth by the improvement of living and sanitary conditions, partly by the regress of the birth-rate. Since the turn of the century the rate of the persons over 60 continuously grew: in the past 25 years this process has accelerated, – as against the 8 per cent of the turn of the century it was 11 per cent in 1941 and 16 per cent in 1968. Also the future continuation of this trend is to be expected, following which also the rate of the older (40–60 years old) persons of productive age will increase at the expense of the younger adults and those in childhood, besides that of the persons over 60 years of age.

The socio-economic effects of senescence are generally known. The number of the pensioners increased from the 560,000 of the year 1952 to 1,270,000 by 1968, the amount of the pension paid grew 11-fold during the same period. In spite of the fact that the pension-fund forms a continuously growing part of the national income, the living-standard of the old is to a considerable degree inferior to that of the productive age-groups and – besides the joint family – it is the aged persons who are the most problematic layer of the population in respect of social policy at present. Although, following the socialist transformation of agriculture, as well as owing to the amendment of the legal statutes referring hereto, the number of pensioners has markedly increased, there are still old-age strata without a pension: about 30,000 of these receive regular social political assistance. The amount of the pensions, primarily for the persons retired some time ago, is relatively small. The situation of about 40 per cent of the pensioners, who keep house jointly with younger members of their family is more favourable; however, the old persons living on low pensions and by themselves, have to depend either on the assistance of their families or on other supplementary income.

Table 10

The age-structure of the population

Age-group years old	Number (thousand persons)					Distribution (per cent)				
	of the population									
	1941	1949	1960	1963	1968	1941	1949	1960	1963	1968
–14	2,420	2,290	2,529	2,474	2,270	26	25	25	25	22
15–39	3,787	3,570	3,662	3,640	3,729	40	39	37	36	37
40–59	2,112	2,272	2,397	2,465	2,558	23	25	24	24	25
60–	997	1,073	1,373	1,493	1,679	11	11	14	15	16
Altogether	9,316	9,205	9,961	10,072	10,236	100	100	100	100	100

The situation of the pensioners is being improved by the process of continuous decrease in the number of the lower pensions set under old legal statutes:

the amount of the pensions fixed under new legal statutes is higher.

Still, the situation of the retired is worsened by the circumstance that – contrary to the continuous increase of the wages, surpassing in their pace the rise of the prices – the amount of their allowance, established at the time of their retirement as a fixed sum, does not change. As a consequence of this, in the long run the real value of the pension decreases. Just for this reason, in the long-term planning the suggestion was made that the amount of the pension should be brought into relation with the wage or price indexes in order that the divergence appearing between the living conditions of the productive and old-age layers could be decreased. The high and continuously rising rate of old-age population expressively points to the necessity to facilitate as much as possible the moment of passing over from the productive age-groups of society to old-age population, a moment problematic in both psychological and economic regard, and to ensure for the old-aged a manner of life free from major disturbances.

Another, less generally known change in the structure of the population ensued from the *family status*. The rate of those married has significantly risen within the full-age population in the last 25 years. This was caused not only by the circumstance that the marrying age has been somewhat shifted toward youth but, in the first place, that the number of definitively unmarried persons has significantly decreased. For instance, 18 per cent of the men and 14 per cent of the women between 30 and 39 years of age were unmarried in 1941. These rates decreased from 15 per cent of the year 1949 to 7 per cent by 1968 with men, and from 12 to 6 per cent with the women in the same period.

In connection with this theme, the rise of the number and proportion of divorced during the past 20–25 years is generally known. Less known, however, is the circumstance that all this hardly influenced the distribution by family-status of the population, since the majority of divorces were followed by remarriages. Thus, although the number of the divorced has increased, their rate in the total population is still rather low (3 per cent).

One of the characteristic processes of our society, significant in its demographic consequences, was that intense birth-control spread rapidly, which on the one hand decreased the number of births, and made general the one- and two-child types of family on the other.

In connection with birth-control, it should be stressed that, contrary to public belief, the proportion of childless married couples was never so low yet as in our days. In 1968, for instance, only 6 per cent of the 30–39 years old married women was childless, which means that the rate of the definitively childless marriages is practically identical with the estimated proportion of the biologically barren women. In other words: complete and conscious refusal of the idea of having children is most infrequent. At the same time the system of families with one child or two children is generally practised, partly by means

EGON SZABADY

Table 11

Trends of the live-birth, death, and natural increase rates

Year	Births	Deaths	Natural increase
	by thousand inhabitants		
1938	19.9	14.2	5.7
1945	18.7	23.4	−4.7
1946	18.7	15.0	3.7
1947	20.6	12.9	7.7
1948	21.0	11.6	9.4
1949	20.6	11.4	9.2
1950	20.9	11.4	9.5
1951	20.2	11.7	8.5
1952	19.6	11.3	8.3
1953	21.6	11.7	9.9
1954	23.0	11.0	12.0
1955	21.4	10.0	11.4
1956	19.5	10.5	9.0
1957	17.0	10.5	6.5
1958	16.0	9.9	6.1
1959	15.2	10.5	4.7
1960	14.7	10.2	4.5
1961	14.0	9.6	4.4
1962	12.9	10.8	2.1
1963	13.1	9.9	3.2
1964	13.1	10.0	3.1
1965	13.1	10.7	2.4
1966	13.6	10.0	3.6
1967	14.6	10.7	3.9
1968	15.1	11.2	3.9

of birthcontrol, partly through legal abortion. In view of the copious literature on this question, the author does not intend to enlarge upon a closer analysis of the subject in this study. It can be factually porved that the development of economy, social regrouping, the rise in the cultural level, the employment of women and several other elements of modern social development had a role in the process of the fall of birth-rate which began at the end of the last century and specially intensified in the past 15 years.

By the way, the high rate of married persons and families having children clearly indicates that although the traditional forms of the family and the content of family-life have changed, the family has not lost its significance either in respect of the individuals or in that of society. It is still the fundamental cell of our society, and its increase and – considering the gradual drop in the number of illegitimate births – nearly exclusive part in reproduction should be especially stressed.

Although the community attends to an ever growing number of tasks in modern society, the most important means of acquiring the knowledge needed for living together in society, for so-called socializing, is still the family.

On the one hand this circumstance underlines the importance of the measures taken for the protection of families hitherto. The significance of the child-care allowance already mentioned is emphasized in this respect by the fact that in the year 1967 the traditional proportion of fecundity of the women who earned their livelihood themselves and those who were being supported changed for the first time, and it was with the earners where a somewhat higher birth-rate appeared. Relying on the results obtained so far, the further development and extension of the institutions of similar character, proved useful in respect of population policy and family protection alike, seems justified also in fields where their effects appeared but to a lesser degree so far (for instance in agriculture).

In connection with the family protection also the problem of compensating the expenses involved in a larger family should be mentioned, the unsatisfactory regulation of which had a significant part in the fall of the birthrate. The amount of the family allowance was exceedingly low at the early 1950s. After several rises of considerable measure, at present it covers about 20–30 per cent of the expenses allotted to the maintenance of children in families with two of more children. Together with the not duly differentiated wages policy, this contributed to the development of a situation in which the living standard of the family was influenced to a greater measure by its demographic structure than by the work done by its head. Neither social not population-political respects justify the maintenance of this; therefore one of the fundamental questions among the long-range aims of social policy is to ensure an adequate compensation of the expenses involved in the support of families.

About the structure, changes and mobility of our society – in the first place in respect of demography – we have at disposal numerical data for over hundred years. In the light of these it can be stated that the last 25 years, the era of our socialist transformation, were the most dynamic period of our history in modern times. This is unequivocally reflected by the mortality indices, sensitive to the changes in social conditions (for instance infant mortality, TB mortality), by the data concerning the structure of economy and of the settlements, the cultural standard, the processes of mobility, etc. which all agree in presenting a picture of a rapidly progressing, rising society in the period under examination.

The progress of economy – the rise of the level of the national income and consumption – as well as the effect of the cultural revolution have essentially determined and favourably influenced social transformation. At the same time, when studying the data, one also meets with phenomena which indicate that in spite of the vast changes, the elements surviving as traditions or as consequences of society's moments of inertia still have an important part in our social reality.

Or course, the preservation of traditions, the continuity of the forms of social behaviour are not to be objected against in themselves. However, they become problematic as continuity is manifested concerning the negative phenomena. It is to be considered unfavourable, e.g. that we still were not able to dispose of our outstanding position as regards the frequency of suicides, prevailing since the turn of the century up to the present. A similar relative constancy can be observed in certain forms of criminality. Although the termination of distress and precariousness of existence of the great masses of the people, the improvement of living conditions have reduced the volume and modified the structure of criminality in certain fields, the relative stability of crimes of emotional background, of violent acts, of crimes against personal safety indicates that asocial tendencies still prevail in the mental attitude and behaviour of considerable social strata. The same can be said also regarding alcoholism, the supporting mass basis of which, though considerably narrowed, is still significant.

It should be noted, further, for completeness' sake, that to ascribe all negative phenomena of our society to a continued operation of detrimental traditions would be a one-sided distortion. It were just the examinations into criminality and alcoholism which referred to the possibility that with the slackening of positive traditions and of the functions of long established social control also the rapid transformation, the high mobility may have their part in the spread of certain forms of behaviour.

This is another example – and numerous others of its kind are to be met with when examining the bordering fields of social science and demography – to demonstrate that positive social processes which are sound in themselves, can have most complex, far-reaching consequences, among which not infrequently also negative phenomena occur.

All this, of course, does not affect the unequivocally positive balance of our 25 years' social changes. Moreover, even the character and dimension of our presentday social problems shed light on many an aspect of the vast progress achieved by us in a quarter of a century. Still, those engaged in the study of social questions should bear in mind the necessity to analyse the processes of the rising societies more minutely and more extensively than this was done up to now, and to examine, besides the basic trends, also the world of details, the wide-ranging processes and multiplying effects of social reality. This is the only way in which they can obtain a full and true picture about the society, in the direction and development of which they are obliged to take part.

BIBLIOGRAPHY

Personal, Family and Housing Data of the Macrocensus of the Year 1968, Central Statistic Office, Budapest, 1969 (p. 78).

Social Regroupment and Its Demographic Effects, *Publications of the Demographic Research Group of the Central Statistic Office*, Budapest, 1965. Vol. 7 (p. 325).

Egon Szabady, Population Changes in Hungary in the Last Twenty Years, *Demográfia*, 1/1965 (pp. 7–19).

Egon Szabady, Economic and Social Consequences of Senescence in Hungary, *Statisztikai Szemle*, 12/1963 (pp. 1055–1062).

Egon Szabady, Contributions to the Regroupment Taken Place in Our Society, *Társadalmi Szemle*, 4/1965 (pp. 134–144).

Egon Szabady, Some Problems of the Position of Women, *Társadalmi Szemle*, 4/1967 (pp. 66–78).

School Attendance and Qualification, *Publications of the Demographic Research Group of the Central Statistic Office*, Budapest, 1967, Vol. 16/2/1967 (p. 105).

Child-care Allowance, *Periodical Statistical Publications*, Central Statistic Office, Budapest, 1969, Vol. 147/13/1969 (p. 98).

Egon Szabady, Making a Living and Motherhood. The Position of Women in Hungary, *The New Hungarian Quarterly*, 34/1969 (pp. 51–63).

Effect of Demographic Factors on Education, *Publication of the Demographic Research Group of the Central Statistic Office*, Budapest, 1967, Vol. 15, 1/1968 (p. 93).

István Kemény, The Social Connections of Mobility, Up-to-date Endeavours of Statistics in Hungary, *Akadémiai Kiadó*, Budapest, 1968 (pp. 502–508).

György Vukovich, The Marriage Mobility of the Three Fundamental Social Strata, *Demográfia*, 3/1963, (pp. 288–314).

Some Lessons to Be Drawn from the Situation of Our Population. (A study compiled within the long-range planning work of the Commission for Planning Labour Force and Living Standards, *Demográfia*, 3–4/1968 (pp. 476–505).

World Views of Population Problems, *Akadémiai Kiadó*, Budapest, 1968 (p. 447).

Alcoholism, *Publications of the Demographic Research Group of the Central Statistic Office*, Budapest, 1968, Vol. 24, 7/1968 (p. 169).

Socio-Economic Changes
and Internal Migration in Bulgaria

IVAN STEFANOV

Sofia

I

INTERNAL migration in many countries has become a very intensive process connected with more or less profound socio-economic changes following World War II. Bulgaria is one of those countries in which industrialization went through a stage of all-round expansion, still continuing with great intensity Prior to World War II industrialization had reached nearly complete stagnation, despite its onesidedness.

On the one hand the classical branches of every industrialization: the food industry, the textile, fur and wood processing industries had reached a level that was believed to be the point of saturation. On the other hand, the official and dominant trend in the country's socio-economic policy was that no conditions existed for the development of heavy industry in Bulgaria. The opinion of progressive economists and economists-Marxists that it is not only possible but also necessary to develop heavy industry collided with the ever more extensively spreading Hitlerite conception of incorporation this country into the Great German economic region as its agricultural, raw material appendage. According to this conception, Bulgaria was to remain an agrarian country with intensive agriculture that would supply the Central European market, dominated by Hitlerite Germany, with fresh and processed farm produce. According to official and semi-official estimates, already after World War I the redundant labour force in Bulgarian agriculture at the then existing technology and farm organization had reached the figure of one million man-years. Experience had shown that intensification of agriculture, with its then existing socio-economic structure, had limited possibilities and was inevitably attended by increase in concealed unemployment in the countryside and by deepening of the class differentiation among the peasantry. In villages where a certain specialization was achieved in the field of tobacco-growing, viticulture, fruit-growing, vegetable, growing, cattle-breeding etc. there were relatively more farms that hired permanent and season labour on the one hand, and comparatively more farms releasing farm labourers for work not only in agriculture but also in industry and the administration, on the other. The hopes of the adherents of the solution of the agrarian question in Bulgaria through intensification of agriculture and cattle-breeding that would strengthen the family-farm were not sustained by the actual developments. Intensification was possible only in some regions and was inevitably attended by deepening of the class differences in the countryside. The family-farm could be maintained as such only in the few cases of medium large farms with a tendency to degrade into small farms or to develop into large farms using hired labour seasonally or permanently.

Still less realistic proved to be the other trend of the socio-economic policy in the period between the two wars: to procure and sell to the farmers large farm equipment and pedigree live stock at reduced prices. This line of development could be followed only by the biggest farms and could bring to the great majority of small and very small farms nothing but ruin. These farms had to resort to other ways.

It is significant that at the height of the big crisis of 1929–1934, in the early 1930's, the first cooperative associations for joint tilling of the land were set up in Bulgaria. Cooperative associations in this country were highly developed in all sectors of the national economy, inclusive of insurance and housing construction, following World War I. This circumstance fostered the shift to the higher form of cooperation – the producers' cooperative with joint tillage of the land and abolition of the boundaries of the individual landed property. The lack of any prospect for the small and medium farms was of decisive importance thereto.

In the beginning of 1947 there were in Bulgaria about one million farms with 4.5 ha of land on the average parcelled into ten plots on the mean, scattered all over the village territory. About two thirds of the farms were small and very small, about one quarter medium and only about one tenth were big peasant and capitalist farms. There was no latifundian land ownership in Bulgaria and nearly all farmers were owners of the land they tilled. The big farmers organized real capitalist farms, using hired labour and machinery. Despite their innate proprietors – sense, the Bulgarian peasants by themselves arrived at the idea of the collective farm, promoted in the USSR at full nationalization of the land (the land in Bulgaria is not nationalized but the land rent is almost completely abolished). After the nationalization of industry and banking in December 1947, real conditions were created for complete planning of the national economy and for accelerated industrialization of all sub-sectors of the economy. First the extractive industry was developed – coal, other fuels, ores and minerals, and ferrous and non-ferrous metallurgy. For centuries these branches of industry had stagnated, but following World War II their output increased by 30, 353 and 418 times resp. compared with 1939.

The output of mechanical engineering at present (1970) is 425 times as high as that of 1939, including most intricate machine's which gained recognition in many developed countries. The chemical and rubber industries also greatly increased their output – by 270 times. Moreover, the classical branches of industry also show unprecedented development: the fur industry – 30 times, textile industry – 21 times, food industry – 14 times and the wood processing industry – 11 times. The total output of industry augmented by 35 times during the same period.

Farm output increased by two times compared with 1939, at diminished

arable area and herds of farm animals. The basic proportion in Bulgarian economy: industry-agriculture underwent a radical change. Prior to World War
II the national income of both sectors was distributed approximately 4:1 in
favour of agriculture while at present this proportion is reversed – 4:1 in favour
of industry.

The second basic proportion – the ratio of light and heavy industry (production of consumer goods and production of producers' goods) also underwent
considerable changes. The share of producers' goods rose from 23 to 53 per cent
while that of consumer goods dropped from 77 to 47 per cent.

II

The tremendous changes in the branch structure of the national economy
resulted in huge migration streams primarily from villages to towns. Such migration from villages to towns existed prior to World War I and even prior to
the end of the 19th century, but the urban/rural population ratio remained
nearly constant – about 1:4 till 1946. The stream from the villages to the
towns hardly compensated the lower natality in the towns, which essentially
determined a lower natural increase in towns and cities. As late as 1947 the
share of the urban population augmented to one fourth and that of the rural
population dropped to three fourths.

In measuring the influence of migration on the urban/rural population
ratio, it is necessary to eliminate the increase in urban population resulting
from the transformation of villages into towns because here there are no population movements, no migration takes place[1]. Urban population increased by the
number of rural inhabitants, the latter not migrating at all. The transformation of villages into towns was much more intensive after World War II than
prior to it. In the 20-year period of 1927–1946 the population in villages transformed into towns amounted to 54 thousand, whereas during the 19-year period
of 1947–1965 it was 576 thousand, i.e. 11 times as much (bearing in mind the
different lengths of the periods).

As early as the beginning of the present century Bulgarian statistics furnish-
ed data on migration through the question of place of birth in the population
censuses (from 1901 to 1934). The average annual migration gain amounted to
(for the intermediate periods):

1901–1905:   7.0 thousand persons
1906–1910: 23.0 thousand persons
1911–1920:   7.5 thousand persons
1921–1926: 38.2 thousand persons
1927–1934: 30.1 thousand persons

---

1 Bulgarian migration statistics includes in migration only permanent migration abroad
   (external migration) or migration from one inhabited place to another (internal migration). Therefore, it does not cover temporary migrations, season migrations, still less pen-
   dulum migration from the place of residence to the place of work.

The relative amount of the migration gain (per thousand inhabitants) ranged from 1.5 to 7.5 per thousand for the 1901–1905 and 1921–1926 periods resp. It is not possible to calculate the migration gain for the period 1934–1946 from data from both successive population censuses on account of World War II.

The average yearly migration gain for the two periods between the last three population censuses (January 1, 1947, December 1, 1956 and 1965) was as follows: for 1947–1956 – 51 thousand persons, for 1957–1965 – 102 thousand. The positive gain is the migration increase of the urban population and the negative one – the decrease due to migration of the rural population. The second period shows twice as large a migration gain as the first one. The relative share of the gain reveals other tendencies owing to the different alteration of the population toward the middle of the periods; urban population increases and rural population declines. That is why despite the two times larger migration gain for the urban population the coefficient rises from 24.1 per thousand to 33.0 per thousand or by 37 per cent while for the rural population the two times bigger negative gain results in a 132 per cent rise of the coefficient.

Bulgarian migration statistics also furnishes data on the migration streams for the same two periods based on the current registration of internal migration (such registration for external migration, of sufficient accuracy, has existed since 1930). The comparison of the migration gains, calculated from census data and current statistics data shows good agreement for the period 1947–1956: the difference is only 4 per cent in favour of the census[2]. The difference reaches 29 thousand or over 29 per cent for the period of 1957–1965. This is due to restrictions on migrations to large cities, which hardly affected the first period. These restrictions were often avaded through fictitious marriages or by granting temporary residence in large cities. Fictitious marriages end by granting residence and the migrant spouse is registered as out-migrant or in-migrant, but through temporary residence thousands of persons live and work for years in one inhabited place but are registered as inhabitants in another place and are not covered by the statistics of internal migration.

From the population census of December 1, 1965 onwards the registration of migrations has been conducted on the basis of registration forms that are filled in on every journey from one inhabited place to another, after elimination of those forms which do not reflect internal migration. The individual information is collected by the organs of the people's militia, which consider this work as rather outside their duties, and that is why so far no sufficiently complete coverage of actual migrations could be ensured. The problem of organizing current statistics of internal migration providing sufficiently complete and de-

---

2 Actually, current statistics should furnish more accurate data on internal migration, for it covers all cases of migration. In calculating the migration gain from data for the factual gain from one census to the next, several kinds of migrations are not covered:
 a. migrations of persons dying before the second census;
 b. repeated migrations are covered only once;
 c. migrations of children born after the previous census.

tailed coverage of migration processes is still not solved, but the Bulgarian Central Statistical Office and Bulgarian statisticians attempt to do this as soon as possible.

The following generalized assessment of the migration streams during the last 24 years – 1947–1970 – is made after thorough verification. The total stream of out-migrants equal to in-migrants accounts for nearly four million persons – 3.961.000 or yearly average of 165.000, which represents 21.3 per thousand. Internal migration is the most intensive demographic process during this period (natality accounting for 17.2 per thousand for the entire period of 1947–1970).

The total stream of out- and in-migrations rapidly increases during the five-year periods of 1951–1955 and 1956–1960, then it levels off at about 160.000 on the average per year, that is, at a level of 35–36 per cent higher than that of 1947–1950 and an average intensity of about 20 per thousand.

The two basic streams – out-migrations from the villages and in-migration to the towns generally run a parallel course with respect to their absolute size. This circumstance shows once again that internal migration is primarily based on the profound and lasting socio-economic changes in Bulgarian society – the intensive and all-round industrialization on the one hand and the socialist reconstruction of agriculture, mainly by cooperation of the peasants, on the other.

The first process resulted in an increased need of labour in industry and the second set free additional labour force (in addition to the concealed unemployment prior to World War II). It cannot be stated that the development of these two processes was always synchronized, but the difference was always brief. Internal migration also had to meet the increased demands of other sectors of social life associated with the reconstruction of the administration of the new state as well as the increased demand for labour in other sectors of the national economy, including the sectors outside the sphere of material production.

III

Detailed data on the absolute size of the migration streams are not adduced, on account of the inaccuracy in the coverage of internal migration by current statistics explained above. This inaccuracy affects less the coefficients-measures of the intensity of migration streams. More detailed data concerning the four basic streams are presented in Tab. 1.

One of the most essential peculiarities of internal migration in Bulgaria is the equal participation of both sexes. In many cases there ubdoubtedly is a certain difference in time in the migration of males and females from one and the same household or family, but this lag affects only a small portion of the migrants and is comparatively quickly overcome. Neither the sex ration of the migrants nor that of those remaining in towns and villages is affected.

The second peculiarity is the considerable decentralization of internal

Table 1

Intensity of the general migration streams

Streams	1947–1950	1951–1955	1956–1960	1961–1965	1966–1970
	Coefficients – per thousand of respective population				
Out-migrants from:					
villages	15.9	20,3	26.0	27.1	25.8
towns	17.9	15.7	10.0	9.0	12.3
In-migrants to					
villages	9.7	9.8	11.5	11.4	9.1
towns	35.4	40.9	37.2	32.1	30.3
Total: out-migrants–in-migrants:	16.4	18.9	20.4	19.8	19.3
Migration gain in:					
towns	6.2	10.5	14.5	15.7	16.7
villages	17.5	24.5	27.2	23.2	18.0
	Development – indices 1947–1950 = 100.0				
Out-migrants from:					
villages	100.0	127.7	163.5	170.4	162.3
towns	100.0	87.7	55.9	50.3	68.7
In-migrants to					
villages	100.0	101.0	118.5	117.5	93.8
towns	100.0	113.5	105.1	90.7	85.6
Total: out-migrants–in-migrants:	100.0	115.2	124.4	120.7	117.7
Migration gain in:					
towns	100,0	160.4	233.9	253.2	269.4
villages	100.0	140.0	155.4	132.6	102.9

migration in Bulgaria. Only mobility over long distances – within the same district; to neighbouring districts and to other districts – can be measured. Bulgaria has 28 districts of an average population of about 290.000 persons Up to 1965 (data are available only for the period from 1960 on all the migrations took place within the boundaries of these extremely small administrative units. In recent years migrations within the same district are decreasing by nearly 16 per cent, constituting, nevertheless, 48 per cent. The number of migrations between neighbouring districts increases gradually but steadily and in recent years constitutes 26 per cent. Migrations within one and the same and neighbouring districts still take up nearly three fourths of all the migrations in recent years against 83 per cent for the period of 1960–1962. On the other hand, mobility over longer distances increased absolutely by almost 40 per cent, accounting for over one fourth of all the migrations.

The ever increasing concentration of economic activity and centralization of administration will also impose a growing centralization of internal migration to the merging, economic, cultural and administrative centres, which, considering this country's conditions, are numerous. On the other hand technical progress limits to a growing extent the extensive development of the economy and the releasing of labour force from farming will lead in the not distant future to further reduction of working time. The complete development of the agricultural-industrial (agroindustrial) complexes will play a major role in this respect. They will attract highly qualified labour on the one hand and will release to a larger extent labour of low or medium qualification.

Table 2

Intensity of migrations according to administrative district

	1960–1962	1963–1965	1966–1970
Coefficients per thousand of respective population			
Within the same district	11.6	12.3	9.3
In neighbouring district	4.5	4.9	5.0
In other district	3.7	3.4	5.0
Total	19.8	20.6	19.3
Development – Indices 1960–1962 = 100.0			
Within the same district	100.0	106.0	80.2
In neighbouring district	100.0	108.0	111.1
In other district	100.0	91.9	135.1
Total	100.0	104.5	97.5
Structure			
Within the same district	58.6	59.7	48.3
In neighbouring district	22.5	23.7	26.0
In other district	18.9	16.6	25.7
Total	100.0	100.0	100.0

The lack of excessive centralization of internal migration is manifested in the fact that less than 11 per cent of the total population reside permanently in Sofia (in 1970, but prior to 1960 less than 10 per cent).

The comparatively small centralization of internal migration in Bulgaria is due to the systematically carried out socio-economic policy to provide livelihood for the population in all districts of the country by setting up industrial enterprises in medium, and even small, towns. In recent years conditions were created to attract tourists, especially from abroad, to small towns and even villages with favourable locations, old monuments and beautiful scenery. It is true that a more or less extensive depopulation of a large number of small villages, or even the complete liquidation of many of them is forthcoming, but the new concentration of agriculture and the adoption of commercial methods in its branches will retain the necessary qualified personnel within the boundaries of the present districts. The constant tendency toward ever increasing concentration of economic activity is a powerful factor contributing to further, more intensive agglomeration of population in a smaller number of centres and it may not always be possible to achieve satisfactory decentralization of the migration streams.

Again from 1960 onwards a more detailed follow-up can be made of the migration streams through combining the directions from and the inhabited places. This results in another four streams: from villages to towns and to villages and from towns to villages and to towns. Use is made of data for three-year periods with a view to avoiding the year-to-year fluctuations. Here again the first place is taken by the stream from the villages directed to the towns, numbering more than one half of all the migration cases, and showing a certain tendency toward increase both in absolute number and in its share. In the beginning of the decennial period migration from villages to villages takes on second place. The importance of this stream was determined by the migration from small villages to central villages. Then this stream accounted for nearly one third of the internal migration. It heavily declined subsequently, and by 1966 ceded the second place to the stream from towns to towns, which increases throughout the whole decennial period, both absolutely and relatively. The stream from towns to villages is the smallest but it shows a distinct tendency toward increase both with respect to its absolute size and its share. This development indicates a migration of highly qualified workers and diverse specialists from the towns to the villages[3].

Bulgarian demographic statistics furnish data on migration from and to each town separately from 1946 onwards. First of all, it should be noted that only *individual, mostly small towns,* have a negative migration gain. The towns are grouped according to two separate characteristics: sized according to the number of their inhabitants and according to their position in the economic/administrative system of the country. Five groups are differentiated by the first characteristic: very small – under 5.000 inhabitants, small – from 5.001 to 10.000, medium, – from 10.001 to 25.000, large – from 25.001 to 100.000 and very large – over 100.000 inhabitants. Five groups are again formed on the basis of the second characteristic: Sofia, 4 very big cities, 9 old district centers under 100.000 inhabitants, 13 new district centers (since 1956) and all remaining towns. Both characteristics may be combined for the last two groups and especially for the last one, in order to obtain more homogeneous groups of towns, but this is still not done.

The migration gain is positive for all groups of towns by both characteristics. The intensity of in-migrations is highest in the large cities. It is only during the first period – 1947–1950 – that the very small towns take up first place with 46 per thousand, which shows that the then dominant migration was from villages to the nearest small towns. In recent years the intensity of migrations to the smallest towns again heavily increases (41 per thousand, against 28 per

---

3   Bearing in mind the aforesaid concerning the inaccuracy of current statistics data, it should be inferred that only the streams from towns to villages and from villages to villages are not affected or are affected less by the factors accounting for this inaccuracy.

Table 3

Intensity of streams from and to inhabited places

Streams		1960–1962	1963–1965	1966–1970
Coefficients – per thousand of respective population				
From villages:				
to towns	a)	25.9	25.4	21.6
	b)	−16.0	−19.5	−19.9
to villages		±10.6	±10.1	±5.8
From towns:				
to villages	a)	−2.7	−1.8	−3.5
	b)	1.6	1.4	3.3
to towns		±6.4	±7.3	±8.7
Migration gain:				
villages-towns	a)	23.2	23.6	18.1
	b)	−14.4	−18.1	−16.6
Development-Indices 1960–1962 = 100,0				
From villages:				
to towns	a)	100,0	98.1	83.4
	b)	100.0	−121.9	−122.2
to villages		100.0	95.3	54.7
From towns:				
to villages	a)	100.0	−66.7	−137.0
	b)	100.0	87.5	206.2
to towns		100.0	114.0	135.9
Migration gain:				
vittages-towns	a)	100,0	101.7	78.0
	b)	100.0	74.3	84.7

Note: The letters *a* (for towns) and *b* (for villages) designate coefficients of streams equal in size to various populations in the middle of the periods (urban and rural). In streams from villages to villages and from towns to towns not only the numerators but also the denominators are the same and that is, why they differ only by their signs (+) or (−).

thousand from the period of 1961–1965). The very big cities have a relatively high intensity of in-migrations only for the period of 1951–1955 – 42 per thousand.

The smallest towns have the highest intensity of out-migrations. This confirms the hypothesis that out-migrations from villages take place first to the small and very small towns and thence to the larger towns. The intensity of out-migrations from the largest cities is very small. Big cities have comparatively low out-migration intensity. Since 1956 the intensity of out-migrations is also small for the group of medium towns.

The migration gain has its *proper development,* for it is the result of in-and-out migrations. The large and very large cities have intensive migration gain at limited intensity of out-migrations. Conversely, in the case of small and very small towns, which have intensive in-migrations but also intensive out-migra-

Table 4

Intensity of in-migrations by groups of towns in numbers of inhabitants

Groups of towns	1947–1950	1951–1955	1956–1960	1961–1965	1966–1970
	Coefficients – per thousand of respective population				
under 5,000	45.7	28.3	35.6	28.4	40.9
5,001– 10,000	40.6	33.8	46.9	36.4	29.2
10,001– 25,000	38.7	35.7	44.3	30.3	25.8
25,001–100,000	36.9	43.2	51.3	38.9	37.8
over 100,000	27.4	41.5	19.9	24.6	25.5
Total	35.4	39.1	37.9	31.8	30.4
	Development – Indices 1947–1950 = 100.0				
under 5,000	100.0	61.9	77.9	62.1	89.5
5,001– 10,000	100.0	83.3	115.5	89.7	71.9
10,001– 25,000	100.0	92.2	114.5	78.3	66.7
25,001–100,000	100.0	117.1	139.0	105.4	102.4
over 100,000	100.0	151.5	72.6	89.8	93.1
Total	100.0	110.5	107.1	89.8	85.9

tions, the intensity of the migration gain is comparatively low, especially so for the very small towns. The migration gain of the large cities is not only most intensive but also most stable.

The sharp decline of the intensity for the very big cities during the 1956–

Table 5

Intensity of out-migrations by groups of towns in numbers of inhabitants

Groups of towns	1947–1950	1951–1955	1956–1960	1961–1965	1966–1970
	Coefficients – per thousand of respective population				
under 5,000	35.2	28.9	30.1	20.3	34.7
5,001– 10,000	25.9	26.5	25.2	21.6	18.7
10,001– 25,000	22.8	22.2	15.9	13.1	15.1
25,001–100,000	17.7	17.1	10.1	9.4	12.9
over 100,000	7.6	3.6	2.2	2.0	6.7
Total	17.8	15.3	10.3	8.5	11.7
	Development – Indices 1947–1950 = 100.0				
under 5,000	100.0	82.1	85.5	57.7	98.6
5,001– 10,000	100.0	102.3	97.3	83.4	72.2
10,001– 25,000	100.0	97.4	69.7	57.5	66.2
25,001–100,000	100.0	96.6	57.1	53.1	72.9
over 100,000	100.0	47.4	28.9	26.3	88.2
Total	100.0	90.0	57.9	47.8	65.7

IVAN STEFANOV

Table 6

Intensity of migration gain by groups of towns in numbers of inhabitants

Groups of towns	1947–1950	1951–1955	1956–1960	1961–1965	1966–1970
	Coefficients – per thousand of respective population				
under 5,000	10.6	0.6	5.5	8.1	6.2
5,001– 10,000	14.6	7.3	21.1	14.8	10.5
10,001– 25,000	15.8	13.5	29.4	17.2	10.7
25,001–100,000	19.2	26.1	41.3	29.4	24.9
over 100,000	19.7	37.9	17.7	22.6	18.8
Total	17.6	23.8	27.6	23.3	18.7
	Development – Indices 1947–1950 = 100.0				
under 5,000	100.0	5.7	51.9	76.4	58.5
5,001– 10,000	100,0	50,0	144.5	101.4	71.9
10,001– 25,000	100,0	85.4	186.1	108.9	67.7
25,001–100,000	100.0	135.9	215.1	153.1	129.7
over 100,000	100.0	192.4	89.8	114.7	95.4
Total	100.0	135.2	156.8	132.4	106.3

1960 period and the attendant steep increase in the intensity of the gain for all other groups of towns is of particular interest. This development can be explained only as a result of the increased severity of the prohibition to grant residence in large and very large cities. On the other hand, these restrictions caused an increase in the gain intensity in all remaining groups of towns.

Sofia, the most important economic and administrative centre of the country has occupied a very particular position since 1956. All migration processes lose a large portion of their former intensity, first of all out-migrations, which, however, have again been intensified to a certain degree in recent years.

Table 7

Intensity of migration streams to and from the city of Sofia

Streams	1947–1950	1951–1955	1956–1960	1961–1965	1966–1970
	Coefficients – per thousand of respective population				
In-migrants	29.7	38.5	13.7	12.2	16.7
Out-migrants	7.4	2.6	1.3	1.0	5.2
Migration gain	22.3	35.9	12.4	11.2	11.5
	Development – Indices 1947–1950 = 100.0				
In-migrants	100.0	145.1	46.1	41.1	56.2
Out-migrants	100.0	35.1	17.6	13.5	70.3
Migration gain	100.0	161.0	55.6	50.2	51.6

Table 8

Intensity of migration streams by groups of cities by their economic-administrative status

Streams	1947-1950	1951–1955	1956–1960	1961–1965	1966–1970
	I. *Large cities, old district centres, 14 cities* *Coefficients – per thousand of respective population*				
In-migrants	30.6	45.5	35.0	40.2	39.1
Out-migrants	12.0	8.5	4.6	3.6	8.5
Migration gain	18.6	37.0	29.4	36.6	30.6
	Development – Indices 1947–1950 = 100.0				
In-migrants	100.0	149.7	111.8	132.2	118.8
Out-migrants	100.0	70.8	37.1	29.0	68.5
Migration gain	100.0	201.1	159.8	198.9	150.0
	II. *Other old district centres (9 cities)* *Coefficients – per thousand of respective population*				
In-migrants	44.9	44.5	57.6	40.9	41.9
Out-migrants	24.0	21.8	10.6	8.8	11.7
Migration gain	20.9	22.7	47.0	32.1	30.9
	Development – Indices 1947–1950 = 100.0				
In-migrants	100.0	99.1	128.3	91.1	93.3
Out-migrants	100.0	90.8	44.2	36.7	48.8
Migration gain	100.0	108.6	224.8	153.6	147.8
	III. *New district centres (14 cities)* *Coefficients – per thousand of respective population*				
In-migrants	40.7	40.9	50.5	37.1	41.2
Out-migrants	24.3	21.6	11.4	8.7	13.3
Migration gain	16.4	19.3	39.1	28.4	27.9
	Development – Indices 1947–1950 = 100.0				
In-migrants	100.0	100.5	124.7	91.2	101.2
Out-migrants	100.0	88.9	46.9	35.8	54.7
Migration gain	100.0	117.7	238.4	173.2	170.1
	IV. *Total remaining cities (not the present district centres)* *Coefficients – per thousand of respective population*				
In-migrants	35.8	37.7	34.8	30.5	29.6
Out-migrants	22.9	26.9	15.8	16.2	20.4
Migration gain	12.9	10.8	19.0	14.3	9.2
	Development – Indices 1947–1950 = 100.0				
In-migrants	100.0	105.3	97.0	85.2	82.7
Out-migrants	100.0	117.5	90.0	70.7	89.1
Migration gain	100.0	83.7	147.3	110.8	71.3

Specific for Sofia is, that the period of 1951–1955 shows greatest intensity of in-migrations (together with the four old big cities). During all the remaining periods Sofia has the smallest intensity of in-migrations, while the old large cities retain their intensity at a higher level than that of the initial period. The development of migrations to and from Sofia leads to the lowest intensity of the migration gain in comparison with all the remaining groups of towns.

The four big cities have a more favourable migration development than the remaining two groups of present district centres. On the one hand in-migrations remain of high intensity and, on the other hand, out-migrations preserve low intensity. Inmigration intensity shows more favourable development at a generally lower level because the initial period (1947–1950) exhibits a comparatively low intensity. The migration gain maintains a comparatively high intensity.

The remaining two groups of present district centres have, on the whole, similar intensity of migration processes at lower intensity of the migration gain. Comparatively low intensity of in-migrations and of the migration gain and high intensity of out-migrations are characteristic of all the remaining cities now not district centres. This circumstance supports the hypothesis of the three-stage character of internal migration: first to central villages, thence to the small and medium towns and finally to the big cities and to the new economic centres engaged in big projects calling for capital investments.

This three-stage character of migration refers actually to a certain portion of the migration streams, while the other and larger portion, passes only through two stages or even only one: from the small village directly to the medium or big town, from the central village directly to the big or very big city, from the small town to the medium and big town, etc.

IV

These are the outlines of actual internal migration in Bulgaria. What are the prospects? The answer to this question was supplied by a statistical survey extremely interesting with regard to its organization, program and techniques (in the form of a sampling survey of the wishes of village youth) carried out in 215 villages, covering 11.250 boys and girls[4]. The object of this sampling survey was to measure the so-called potential out-migration of village youth and the effect of the factors determining it. It turned out that 44 per cent of the youth are determined to leave the village in which they live and in which most of them

---

4   The sample was taken on stochastic principles, on cluster basis and covered all youths (of ages ranging from 16 to 28 last birthday) in villages selected at random. The general characteristic of the villages is sketched by a special questionnaire. Each boy (girl) filled in a sampling survey form without writing, merely underlining the suitable answers to all questions. Real and complete anonymity of the information was ensured, without which there could be no frank information on many questions concerning youth. The registration was carried out in the latter half of May, 1967 (immediately before the rush-season farm work). See coll. "Socialism and Youth", Sofia, 1969, p. 229.

were born. This is a really very alarming prospect both for the future rural population and for accomodation of migrants to towns.

Indeed youth out-migration will disturb still more the age, and partially, the sex structure of rural population. It will accelerate the ageing of that population and will create additional grounds for out-migration of youth. The results of the sampling survey – a typical sociological study – show that potential migration is more intensive in the case of better educated and trained youth. These results also give some grounds for outlining and carrying out such socio-economic policy as will regulate the forthcoming migration streams from villages to towns, because they measure the effect of the decisive assessment of youth concerning their position and behaviour. Moreover, information is collected concerning the basic elements of the value system itself of village youth.

It is not possible to enumerate here all the factors for village youth out-migration covered by the survey. We shall merely indicate their groups:

1. Type of village: central, the seat of the people's country council and the adjacent villages belonging to the same county on the one hand and distance to the town most frequented by youth on the other. The potential migration in the more distant adjacent villages accounted for 54 per cent, i.e. 23 per cent higher than the total potential migration, while those determined to stay in the village account for only 26 per cent. The corresponding figures for the central and close to the town villages are 36 per cent and 39 per cent resp.
2. Dissatisfaction of youth with cultural life in the village: music performances, cinemas, theatrical performances, available books, lectures, talks, sports facilities, dancing halls.
3. Problems related to the occupational activities of youth: availability of suitable jobs in the village and in the town, adequate pay, organization of labour, quality of leadership and relations in the labour collective.
4. Problems of love, of the young family, and personal happiness of youth, principally, the idea of the opportunities for the more radical solution of these problems in the village and in the town, which is affected by many other factors, as for instance, education, marital status, children born and their number, etc.

There is a very large number of small villages and even hamlets – about 5.500 – in Bulgaria. Some of them lack "potential out-migration" because of the lack of youth. The sampling survey, indicated above, could not cover about 15 per cent of the envisaged villages owing to absence of youth in them. There are, however, villages having only a few inhabitants or even completely depopulated. Undoubtedly, in the next ten years or so a considerable number of villages, precisely the smallest and farthest away from the centres of economic, cultural and political life, will be liquidated.

Function specialization will be carried out in the remaining villages. Some of them will become residential areas for those working in the near-by town.

Some of the small towns will also assume such a function. Other villages will develop as centres for rest, recreation and medical treatment of the working people or as centres of international tourism or for both purposes simultaneously of consecutively. Specialization will also affect the sectors of the national economy. The same basic lines of specialization may be foreseen for the small and some very small towns.

In all categories of inhabited places that are to remain permanent, conditions should be created to satisfy the needs of the whole population and especially of youth so as to limit migration to the socially necessary extent. Furthermore, they should be conformed to the conditions and possibilities of the inhabited places from and to which the migration streams are directed. Socialist society has all the possibilities to carry out successfully such regulation of internal migration.

V

Conclusion. Following World War II Bulgaria had to overcome two big lags in the development of its economy: one-sided industrialization (with rudimentary development of heavy industry and comparatively small capitalist enterprises and a great number of artizan shops) and parcelling of farm holdings (4.5 ha tilled land on the average, parcelled into 10 plots on the mean), primitive technology and concealed unemployment. Within two decades of recovery development Bulgaria was transformed from a backward agrarian country into an industrial-agrarian one. This was achieved by means of expanded all-round industrialization at high rates and socialist reconstruction of agriculture, mainly through cooperation of the peasants in big farms, supplied with modern machinery, certified seed, pedigree live stock, artificial fertilizers and chemicals for disease and pest control, commercial methods of production and organization and steady concentration. The cooperation of peasants in big farms was deeply rooted in the traditions of the early 1930's, based on the highly developed cooperative associations and the experience of kolkhoz farmers in the USSR.

The intensive and radical reorganization of Bulgarian society after World War II caused great expansion of internal migration. Especially intensive were and still are the out-migrations from villages and in-migrations to towns – about 26 and over 30 thousand persons of the respective population on the average per year. Internal migration in Bulgaria is characterized by the balance of the sexes and great, recently decreasing, decentralization. Nevertheless, still three quarters of the whole internal migration, and up to 1966 over four fifths, occurred in the small administrative units – the districts (of 290.000 inhabitants on the average) – and between adjacent districts.

On account of the strict prohibition to grant residence in large and very large cities, big towns of 25–100.000 inhabitants have the greatest attraction power, and the capital – Sofia – least. The out-migration intensity is highest in the small and smallest towns. It is again the large cities that have the highest intensity of migration gain and the smallest towns the lowest.

It is reasonable to assume that a portion of internal migration passes through three stages: from small villages to central ones, thence to small and the smallest towns and thence to big cities and the capital, the in-migrations of which are of least intensity, the out-migrations likewise being least intensive.

Considerable decrease in the number of villages should be expected, as well as specialization in the development of villages and small (and smallest) towns to meet definite social wants (even more concentrated economic activity, residence for those working in near-by centres of economic activity, recreation, medical treatment and health improvement, international tourism, etc.)

It may be expected that the possibilities will be increased of regulating internal migration within the range necessary for the development of society and in the interest of the working people, by avoiding excessive out-migration from firmly established inhabited places and overburdening of other inhabited places with unnecessary in-migrants.

Mortality Trends in the
Socialist Countries of Eastern Europe
after World War II[1]

EGON SZABADY

Budapest

IN the years after World War II the decrease of mortality – in the socialist countries of Eastern Europe – which started at the turn of the century – took a sudden change. In the last 20–25 years the mortality of the region's population improved at an exceedingly quick rate. It decreased at a relatively uniform but moderate rate already in the decades proceding World War II, although according to G. Stolnitz [1] even this rate was considerably higher than that experienced in the countries of Western Europe in the corresponding stage of their development. Beside this quick rate of decrease the post-war trend – covering more than two decades – can also be characterized by its wide spread (affecting almost all countries of the region), by the decrease of the earlier important interregional differences, by the considerable decrease of the differences between urban and rural mortality, and, not in the least, by the remarkable convergency of mortality in Eastern and in Western Europe where it had attained a low level already earlier.

When analysing the mortality trends of Eastern Europe the impacts of the two World Wars should by all means be taken into account, as they caused immense population losses in the countries in question (especially World War II should be mentioned here). As a direct result of the war events almost 30 million people died in the region during World War II, including also Germany. Moreover, it is also well known that the food and public health situation, which deteriorated as a result of the war, affected similarly, first of all, the population of the socialist countries of Eastern Europe and contributed considerably to the increase of mortality. Their unfavourable demographic impact could be experienced for a long time. [2]

A joint analysis of mortality in the socialist countries of Eastern Europe is justified, first of all, by the common features of the mortality trends in the last decades, indicated above. These countries are: Albania, Bulgaria, Czechoslovakia, Jugoslavia, Poland, Hungary, the German Democratic Republic, Roumania and the Sovjet Union. The data referred to in the text relate to the

---

1   This paper was prepared for the Demographic Symposium held in Varna, Bulgaria, between 25–30 September, 1968.

period preceding World War II and to the populations living in the area of the countries in the corresponding period. A closer examination of the factors of these trends gives, however, a rather heterogeneous picture. In the period before World War II, there were considerable regional differences in the level and structure of mortality in the countries of the region. The impacts and demographic consequences of the war affected the different countries of the region to a different extent and, at last, great differences manifested themselves with regard to the level of economic development, the population's living-standard, health care etc. Beside the mentioned above common features of the mortality trends of the post-war period, a comprehensive study of mortality in the socialist countries of Eastern Europe is also justified by the similarities that could be experienced in the social and economic transformation of these countries after World War II. In the last decades the quick industrialization, the organization of socialist agricultural production, the establishment of new social relations etc., made it possible to increase the living-standard of the population: the general food and housing conditions etc. improved considerably. The quick improvement of social conditions was greatly promoted by the introduction of the general social insurance and by the quick betterment of the health conditions.

In the socialist countries of Eastern Europe medical treatment and medicine can be obtained free of charge by almost everybody. To make proper use of the existing possibilities the network of public health institutions has been greatly extended. In 1962, the number of physicians per 10,000 of population exceeded 10 (Albania, Jugoslavia and German Democratic Republic excluded), while the number of hospital beds per 10,000 of population was more than 60 (excluding Albania and Jugoslavia) (Table 1). These figures are close to the corresponding data of most West European countries, in fact, they surpass them with regard to the relative number of physicians. Thus, beside the general development of medicine, all these factors have influenced the mortality trends of the region in the same direction [3] and contributed greatly to the quick improvement of the mortality conditions and to the considerable extension of the duration of human life.

The good quality of vital statistics in the region offers a reliable basis for studying mortality conditions in the socialist countries of Eastern Europe. The statistical registration of deaths is almost complete and in the middle of the 1960's (apart from some rural districts in the socialist countries of Southern Europe), the cause of death was ascertained to the extent of almost 100 per cent by a physician, to a great extent by post-mortem examination. The still existing differences in the definition of infant mortality, resulting from the different definitions of live births, raise, however, some problems for a comparison. Regarding the generally accepted definition "Live birth is the complete expulsion or extraction from its mother of a product of conception, irrespective of the duration of pregnancy, which, after such separation, breathes or shows any evidence of life, such as beating of the heart, pulsation of the umbilical cord, or definite movement of voluntary muscles, whether or not the umbilical

Table 1

Number of Physicians and Hospital Beds
per 10,000 Inhabitants in the Socialist Countries of Eastern Europe 1962

Country	Physicians	Hospital beds
Albania	3.2[1]	54[1]
Bulgaria	16.0	61[1]
Czechoslovakia	17.0	101
German Democratic Republic	9.1	121
Hungary	17.1	73
Poland	10.7	69
Roumania	13.4	74
Sovjet Union	21.5	87
Jugoslavia	7.0	46[2]

[1] 1961.
[2] 1962.

cord is been cut or the placenta is attached: each product of such a birth is considered live born", divergence from this definition can be experienced mostly with regard to the interpretation of the concept "sign of life".

In Poland, the German Democratic Republic and Hungary, the existence of one of the evidences of life is required according to the definition, in the Sovjet Union, Bulgaria and Roumania, the existence of one single evidence of life, namely that of breathing is required: finally, in Albania and in Czechoslovakia, the joint existence of several evidences of life is required (breathing and pulsation in Albania, pulsation or movement and breathing of 1 hour in Germany). Besides, in Bulgaria, Czechoslovakia (up to 1964) and the Sovjet Union, there are still additional criteria: namely the length of the foetus has to reach 35 cms, its weight must be over 1,000 grams (except in Bulgaria) and – except in the Sovjet Union – the foetus has to be born after 28 weeks of pregnancy. There are also some differences in the definition of birth. Regarding some socialist countries in Eastern Europe we have no satisfactory data about the completeness of statistical registration. All these differences considerably hinder a regional comparison of infant mortality. At present, we have still no data about mortality on basis of a uniform definition for general use. [4]

The above mentioned improvement of mortality is also reflected in the development of the crude death-rates. In the years immediately following World War II, the number of deaths per 1,000 of population still exceeded 15% in most countries and reached high values especially in the German Democratic Republic and in Roumania (Table 2). In the subsequent period mortality went through a quick and uniform decrease and fell to 10‰ (in 5 of the 9 countries they sank even under this figure) by the end of 50's. As a result, the death-rate decreased to 7.5 % in the Sovjet Union and in Poland, it stabilized between 8–9 % in Bulgaria, Roumania and Jugoslavia and around 10 % in

Czechoslovakia and Hungary, while in Albania there are still greater fluctuations around 10 ‰. The German Democratic Republic is the only country of the region where mortality has increased, in a small degree only, since the early 1950's. It seems to have become stabilized around 13 ‰ in the 60's. Beside the decrease of mortality, the above indicated trends of the crude mortality death-rates are influenced by numerous factors; thus, first of all, by the irregularities of the age-compositions of the populations concerned. The age-compositions of the populations of countries with low mortality – first of all, the age-compositions of Bulgaria, Poland, Roumania, the Sovjet Union and Jugoslavia – are very young (partly due to the heavy population losses during World War II, partly to the high fertility of the post-war period).

The improvement of infant mortality has played an important role in the said decrease of mortality [3]. The exceedingly high infant mortality of the pre-war years, when it passed 160–170 ‰ in Roumania and the Sovjet Union, 140 ‰ in Bulgaria, Poland and Jugoslavia, and was over 130 ‰ even in Hungary and 110–120 ‰ in Czechoslovakia, began to decrease quickly after World War II [2]. In the first 5 year-period after the War mortality was still higher than 100 ‰ in all countries of Eastern Europe (with the exception of Czechoslovakia); it surpassed pre-war infant mortality in the G.D.R. only; at the beginning of the 50's, however, an impressive improvement of infant mortality could be observed in the whole region (Table 1). The quickest decrease could be registered in Czechoslovakia and the G.D.R., but there was also a considerable decrease in Hungary, Roumania and the Sovjet Union. By the 50's infant mortality fell under 100 ‰ in all socialist countries of Eastern Europe and continued to improve at a uniform, quick rate in most countries of Eastern Europe. Only Albania and Jugoslavia form an exception, where the rate of decrease of infant mortality was relatively lower and still high by European standards even in the middle of the 60's [5]. By the middle of the 60's the number of infant deaths per 1,000 live births fell under 45 in the other countries of the region, it did not even reach 30 ‰ in Czechoslovakia, the German Democratic Republic, the Sovjet Union. (It should be noted, however, that the definition of live birth, given under par. 4, is the narrowest in these three countries, where also the cases, regarded as infant deaths in other countries, are ranked among still births.) In 1971, for instance – disregarding those who died within the first hour after birth as well as on the first day due to atelactasis of the lungs, and those who were born with a weight less than 1,000 grams – infant mortality in Hungary would have been 37.7 ‰ instead of the registered 44.1 ‰. At any rate, it can be stated that the former characteristic feature of mortality in Eastern Europe – disregarding those parts of the region which belong to Central Europe – namely the high proportion of infant deaths, has remained an explicit feature of the post-war period, too, though it is perhaps less marked than before [3].

The indices of the life-table, especially the average expectation of life at different ages, offer the best basis for studying the development of mortality. In the period that has elapsed since World War II, 30 published life-tables have

Table 2

Mortality and Infant Mortality in the Socialist Countries of Eastern Europe after World War II

Period	Al-bania	Bul-garia	Czecho-slovakia	G.D.R.	East Berlin	Hun-gary	Poland	Rou-mania	Jugo-slavia	Soviet-Union
Average annual number of deaths per 1000 inhabitants										
1945–49	15.8[1]	13.3	13.6	17.4[1]	19.2[1]	14.5	11.4*[2]	17.5[1]	13.2[2]	–
1950–54	14.3	10.2	10.9	11.7	14.3	11.4	11.1	12.0	12.4	9.1
1955–59	11.4	8.9	9.7	12.4	15.5	10.3	9.0	9.7	10.5	7.7
1960–64	9.8	8.2	9.5	13.1[1]	16.9[1]	10.1	7.6	8.6	9.4*	7.2
1965	9.0	8.0	10.0*	13.4*[3]	–.–	10.7	7.4*	8.6	8.7	7.3
Average annual number of infant deaths per 1.000 live-births										
1945–49	104.1[1]	127.0	91.1[1]	100.2[1]	182.7	114.2	109.1*[4]	159.3[1]	102.1[5]	–.–
1950–54	108.0	93.6	58.2	59.9	59.8	73.8	97.7	105.0	115.7	75
1955–59	83.2	66.1	31.0	45.2	44.4	58.7	74.7	78.0	98.5	47
1960–64	85.3	37.8	22.5	33.8[1]	32.8[1]	44.5	52.6	63.0	81.5	32
1965	86.8	30.8	25.3*[3]	24.5*[3]	–.–	38.8	41.8*	44.1	71.5*	27

*   Preliminary estimated figure.
[1]   Average of 4 years.
[2]   Average of 3 years.
[3]   Including East-Berlin.
[4]   Average of 2 years.
[5]   Only one single year.

Table 3

*Average Expectation of Life at Birth by Sex in the Socialist Countries of Eastern Europe
after World War II*

(years)

Country	Years of the life-tables	Average expectation of life at birth		
		Both sexes[1]	Men	Women
Albania	1950–51	53.49	52.60	54.37
	1955–56	57.89	57.20	58.58
	1960–61	64.85	63.69	66.00
	1963–64	64.85	63.70	66.00
Bulgaria	1956–57	65.91	64.17	67.65
	1960–62	69.59	67.82	71.35
Czechoslovakia	1949–51	63.23	60.93	65.53
	1955	68.70	66.24	71.15
	1960	70.50	67.81	73.18
	1964	70.66	67.76	73.56
German Dem. Republic	1952–53	67.07	65.06	69.07
	1954–55	68.18	66.20	70.15
	1963–64	70.81	68.27	73.34
Hungary	1948–49	61.00	58.75	63.24
	1955	66.92	64.96	68.87
	1959–60	67.38	65.18	69.57
	1964	69.42	67.00	71.83
Poland	1948	59.05	55.6	62.5
	1955–56	64.80	61.8	67.8
	1960–61	67.65	64.8	70.5
Roumania	1956	63.24	61.48	64.99
	1961	65.95	64.19	67.70
	1963	67.80	65.35	70.25
Jugoslavia	1952–54	58.13	56.92	59.33
	1958	64.36	62.87	65.85
	1960–61	63.73	62.18	65.27
	1961–62	64.00	62.41	65.58
Sovjet Union	1958–59	68.05	64.42	71.68
	1964–65	70.00	66.00	74.00

[1] Average value of the expectations of life relating to men and women.

been calculated with regard to the population of the 9 countries of the region.
Thanks to the good quality of the crude mortality data and the age data of the
population censuses these table values possess a high degree of reliability, and
problems are caused only by the different definitions of infant death in various
countries. It is known, for instance, that a 10–15 per cent underestimation of infant mortality may considerably modify the average expectation of life at
birth. Still, the available life-tables offer the most reliable basis for studying
mortality trends.

Accordingly, in the post-war period the average expectations of life at birth did not reach 65 years in the greater part of the region; in fact, in the socialist countries of Southern Europe – perhaps with the exception of Bulgaria – they were under 55 years, and reached the lowest level (53.5 years) in Albania (in 1950–1951). From the early 50's on the average expectations of life at birth started to increase at a rapid rate in the whole region and by the early 60's reached, or came close to, 70 years in most countries of the region (Table 3). By the beginning of the present decade, from among the socialist countries of Eastern Europe, the average expectation of life at birth did not reach 65 years in Albania and Jugoslavia only, and it exceeded 69 years in the other countries of the region with the exception of Poland, where it came to 67.6 years only in 1960/61. It is characteristic feature of the rate of development that the average value of the expectation of life at birth was still 65.8 years in the middle of the 50's, in the first half of the 60's it increased to 69.6 years, i.e. during hardly half a decade it increased by 4 years. Accordingly, in the socialist countries of Eastern Europe, the average expectation of life at birth, which was still low by the European standards after the War, in general came near to or reached at any rate the level in Western Europe by the early 60's, with the exception of Albania and Jugoslavia [1].

An other characteristic feature of the development is – similarly to the former trend in Western Europe – the decrease of the regional differences. While even in the mid-50's the difference between the lowest and highest expectations of life at birth in the region was 10.8 years, at the beginning of the

Table 4

Growth of the Average Expectation of Life at Birth (e⁰) for Both Sexes in the Second Half of the 1950's in the Socialist Countries of Eastern Europe

Country	Period (years of) the life tables	Average increase per 1 year of e° (in years)	Value of e° for both sexes at the beginning of the period	Order by the value of e°
Albania	1955/56–1960/61	1.39	57.9	8
Bulgaria	1956/57–1960/62	0.92	65.9	5
Jugoslavia	1952/54–1960/61	0.75	58.1	9
Poland	1955/56–1960/61	0.57	64.8	6
Roumania	1956–1961	0.54	63.2	7
Czechoslovakia	1955–1960	0.36	68.7	1
Sovjet Union	1958/59–1964/65	0.33	68.1	3
German Dem. Republic	1954/55–1963	0.29	68.2	2
Hungary	1955/59–1960	0.12	66.9	4

60's this difference decreased to 6.9 years. Due to the high mortality in Southern Europe these differences are of considerable importance even today.

One of the characteristic features of the 20th century mortality of Western Europe shown by G. Stolnitz, according to whom the increase of the levels of survival is the quickest in those countries where the former level was relatively lower [1] – can be found also in Eastern Europe. When analysing the 5-year trends in the second half of the 50's, it can be stated that though in this period the average expectations of life at birth already reached relatively high values in the greater part of the region, in most cases the quickest development took place in the countries with a relatively lower average expectation of life – first of all, in Albania, Jugoslavia and Poland while in the countries with low mortality also the increase of the average expectations of life was slower (Table 4). The latter statement refers, first of all, to the German Democratic Republic, the Sovjet Union and Czechoslovakia. This is, however, only an approximate picture of the situation in Eastern Europe, since Bulgaria and Hungary considerably deviate from the general description above. In Belgaria a relatively higher average expectation of life at birth went through a rapid increase at the end of the 50's – it is the second highest value in the region – while in Hungary, the level of the average expectation of life at birth, nearly the same as in Bulgaria, went through an insignificant increase only – it is the lowest in the region –. It would be difficult to give a proper explanation of these two exceptions: they are due, perhaps, to the fact that there are still considerable fluctuations in the level and structure of mortality in subsequent calendar years in the region.

With regard to the mortality by sex, the higher mortality of men prevails in the whole region. Around the 60's the average expectation of life at birth of women exceeded that of men by 5 years on the average (the average value of the differences was 4.9 years, somewhat lower than 15 years earlier). The differences of the average expectations of life at birth are, in general, higher in the countries with low mortality (the highest difference – 7.3 years – is in the Sovjet Union) and lower in the countries with high mortality (Table 5). The lowest value could be found in Albania. (Considering the different regions of the world, for some decades the differences between the average expectations of life at birth have been the greatest in Eastern Europe.) The differences by sex decrease, in general, with advancing age the only exception is Albania where the differences reach their maximum at the age of 30 and decrease to 2–3 years by the age of 60, with the exception of Bulgaria and the Sovjet Union. At any rate, the already mentioned decrease of the average value of the differences in the last decades left the older age groups almost unaffected.

The development of mortality by age will be touched upon here only briefly. The mortality of the older age groups changed relatively slowly in the last two decades, and this is partly reflected in the slow increase of the average expectations of life at older ages. In most countries the average expectation of life at the age of 60 changed only by one year in the last 10–15 years.

After World War II also the distribution of deaths by causes went through

Table 5

Differences by Sex of the Average Expectations of Life at Different Ages (values of females minus values of males) in the Socialist Countries of Eastern Europe Around 1960

(years)

Age years	Country, years of the life tables								
	Albania 1960–61	Bulgaria 1960–62	Czecho- slovakia 1960	G.D.R. 1963–64	Hungary 1959–60	Poland 1960–61	Rou- mania 1963	Jugo- slavia 1960–61	Sovjet- Union 1958–59
0	2.3	3.5	5.4	5.1	4.4	5.7	4.9	3.1	7.3
1	2.9	3.1	5.1	4.7	3.9	5.1	3.6	2.8	7.0
30	3.9	2.6	4.3	3.9	3.3	4.4	3.0	2.9	6.4
60	2.6	1.6	2.7	2.9	2.1	2.8	1.8	2.0	3.6

Table 6

Average Annual Number of Deaths per 100,000 Inhabitants according to Some Leading Causes of Death[1] in Some Socialist Countries of Eastern Europe 1962–1964.

Country	Tuberculosis (B 1-2)	Malignant neoplasms (B 18)	Vascular lesions affecting the central nervous system (B 22)	Heartdiseases (B 25)	Influenza pneumonia (B 30-31)	Gastritis (B 36)	Nephritis and neprozis (B 38)	Congenital malformations and other diseases peculiar to early infancy (B 41-44)	Senility without mention of psychosis, ill-defined and unknown causes (B 45)	Accidents (B 47-48)
				Number of deaths due to						
				per 100,000 inhabitants						
Bulgaria	16.01	130.29	144.16	190.84	81.73	2.35	7.75	30.11	43.17	37.70
Czechoslovakia	18.84	195.88	96.83	225.68	36.52	4.52	6.98	26.16	24.20	44.59
Hungary	27.46	180.44	142.76	285.72	31.82	6.45	7.96	39.54	24.49	39.06
Poland	40.79	112.02	37.01	125.37	52.75	12.00	6.99	45.36	114.89	38.67
Roumania	31.08[2]	213.95[2]	114.18[2]	229.63[2]	84.52[2]	9.54[2]	13.59[2]	33.95[2]	7.80[2]	50.54[2,3]
Jugoslavia	37.30	81.37	63.19	179.69	67.27	19.34	9.89	84.13	237.28	50.52

1 Deaths are coded according to the categories of the Abbreviated List/B/ of the VIIth International Revision of Diseases.
2 1961, 1962, 1965.
3 Including suicides and self-inflictions.

a considerable change in the socialist countries of Eastern Europe. Mortality due to T.B., influenza, pneumonia and gastritis (leading causes of death earlier), has greatly decreased in all countries of the region. At the same time, heart-diseases, cancer and other malignant neoplasms have gained in importance. At present, among the causes of death, heart diseases are on the first place, central nervous system on the third place in all countries of the region. It is a characteristic feature of Bulgaria only that some years ago mortality due to vascular lesion of the central nervous system was higher than that due to malignant neoplasms (Table 6). The change in the structure of deaths by causes of death is partly the result of great progress achieved in fighting down the contagious diseases (once T.B. was a widespread disease in all countries of the region), partly it is connected with the ageing of the region's population, as a result of which the typical diseases of old age, such as heart-diseases and malignant neoplasms, are responsible for a higher number of deaths.

What perspectives would the increase of the average duration of life in the socialist countries of Eastern Europe have if all the so-called exogeneous causes of death were eliminated from mortality? According to the table de mortalité limit [6] of Jean Bourgeois-Pichat, in case of eliminating the exogeneous causes of death, the average duration of life of men would be 76.3 years, that of women 78.2 years, and that of the total population, covering both sexes, 77.2 years [6]. The socialist countries of Eastern Europe are not equally far from reaching these values of the average duration of life. It is clear (Table 7) that in all socialist countries of Eastern Europe, after elimination of these exogeneous causes of death, there is a greater distance to reach these values of the average duration of life for men than for women, in spite of the fact that this value of the average duration of life is more favourable in case of women.

On basis of the available life-tables there is only little possibility to draw conclusions to the actual future development of mortality in Eastern Europe. If we take the recent mortality trends of the countries with low mortality in Western Europe as indicators, then it may be expected that a quick improvement of mortality can be reckoned with in the future, first of all, in the socialist countries of Southern Europe where mortality is still high. Besides, mortality can be improved considerably in Hungary and Poland through a further decrease of infant mortality.

Owing to the limited scope of this paper we could not analyse in detail the mortality of the socialist countries in Eastern Europe from other aspects. As one of our debts we would mention first of all, a deeper analysis of the age-structure and the structure by causes of death of mortality with regard to which research started in the Hungarian Demographic Research Institute previously. There the life table of Hungary's population by causes of death for 1959/60 has been prepared [7], which is of great help in judging the perspective of the future decrease of mortality. As far as we know, life-tables of this type have not been prepared so far in the other socialist countries of Eastern Europe.

In the last 20–25 years, mortality in the socialist countries of Eastern Europe, which decreased at a uniform but moderate rate in the period prior to

Table 7

Possibilities of Growth of the Average Expectation of Life at Birth in the Socialist Countries of Eastern Europe in case the Exogeneous Causes of Death are Eliminated

Country	Years of the life-tables taken as basis for the calculation of the possibilities of growth	Average expectation of life at birth			Growth of the average expectation of life at birth in case the exogeneous causes of death are eliminated		
		Men	Women	Both sexes	Men	Women	Both sexes
Albania	1963–1964	63.70	66.00	64.85	12.60	12.20	12.35
Bulgaria	1960–1962	67.82	71.35	69.59	8.48	6.85	7.61
Czecho-slovakia	1964	67.76	73.56	70.66	6.54	4.64	6.54
German Dem. Republic	1963–1964	68.27	73.34	70.81	8.03	4.86	6.39
Hungary	1964	67.00	71.83	69.42	9.30	6.37	7.78
Poland	1960–1961	64.80	70.50	67.65	11.50	7.70	9.55
Roumania	1963	65.35	70.25	67.80	10.95	7.95	9.40
Jugoslavia	1961–1962	62.41	65.58	64.00	13.89	12.62	13.20
Sovjet-Union	1964–1965	66.00	74.00	70.00	10.30	4.20	7.20

World War II, has improved at an exceedingly rapid rate. The mortality differences between the various countries of the region, between the urban and rural population within the countries, and between Eastern and Western Europe (where it had attained a low level already earlier) have diminished. Of the changes accompanying economic growth it is the health care that has played the greatest role in this rapid improvement (Table 1). The still existing differences in the definition on infant mortality arising from the varying definitions of live birth, are in the way of a more thorough analysis of the mortality differences within the region. The development of the crude birth-rate infant mortality (Table 2) and the average duration of life (Table 3) show a relatively favourable picture after World War II. In the different countries of the region the average duration of life has increased at different rates (Table 4). First of all, it has been rapid in the countries where mortality was relatively unfavourable earlier. In respect of mortality by sex, the higher mortality of men is predominant in the whole region. The differences by sex of the average duration of life, are, in general, higher in the low mortality countries – the highest value could be registered in the Sovjet Union where it was 7.3 years (Table 5). Of the causes of death heart diseases, malignant neoplasms and vascular lesion of the nervous system are the most important (Table 6). In all countries of the region men are farther from the values – estimated by Bourgeois-Pichat – of the average expectation of life after the elimination of the exogeneous causes of death than women, despite the fact that this value of the average duration of life is more favourable among women. (Table 7).

BIBLIOGRAPHY

[1] G. J. Stolnitz, *A century of international mortality trends: I-II*. Population Studies Vol. 9, No. 1, 1955 (pp. 24–55) and Vol. 10, No. 1, 1956 (pp. 17–42).

[2] Milbank Memorial Fund: *Trends and differentials in mortality*, New York, 1956, 165 p.

[3] E. Szabady, *Social and biological factors affecting infant mortality in Hungary*, International population conference, New York, 1961, Tome 1 (pp. 768–776).

[4] Gy. Acsádi, *A népmozgalimi statisztikák nemzetközi egysegesitésének kérdése a KGST orszagok szakértói munkacsoportjának budapesti ülésén*, Demográfia 2, 1964, pp. 266–280.

[5] D. Tasic, *Smrtnost odojcadi u Jugoslaviji, Institut drustvenih nauka*, Beograd, 1966, 286 p.

[6] J. Bourgeois-Pichat, *Essai sur la mortalité "biologique" de l'homme*, Population, No. 3, 1952, (pp. 381–395).

[7] A. B. Lukács, E. Pallós: *A haláloki halandósági táblák számitásának néhány kérdése*, Demográfia, No. 4, 1966 (pp. 441–474).

Migration and Social Change in Europe

JOHN A. JACKSON

Belfast

POPULATION movement has always been an essential ingredient of the process of social change and development. Capital development recruits labour and the processes of industrialisation and urbanisation draw in population from the rural hinterland to the growing urban and industrial centres. The countries of Europe have been regarded in the past as sources of migrants travelling to the New World of the Americas, Australia and the African and Asian colonies of the major European countries. Throughout the second half of the nineteenth century this characteristic migration over the long sea routes emptied Europe of a large surplus pool of peasant labour while extensive 'internal' migrations relocated much of the population that remained in the growing industrial centres. The rate of population growth declined in part because of this not outward balance of migration and in Ireland where it combined with late marriage and a low marriage rate the population actually declined in spite of large family size.

Although this pattern continues in a vestigial form largely sustained by the communities of first, second, third and fourth generation immigrants from Europe settled in the various receiving countries, its significance is now very slight when compared with internal migration within Europe itself and the immigration into European countries of nationals from former colonial or imperial territories. The Netherlands received back 58,000 Dutch citizens from Indonesia and West New Guinea between 1958 and 1962; 815,000 Algerians returned to France between 1962 and 1964.[1] Britain and Belgium are among those which have experienced a similar reverse migration of expatriate nationals and colonial citizens who have claims on the home country. The immigration of West Indian and African workers and their families since the war to Britain has demonstrated the extent and direction of this return flow which typifies the nineteen fifties and sixties.

For most European countries the balance has changed and as their economic growth has made fresh demands on a relatively stable population they have become countries of immigration rather than emigration. The countries of immigration in Europe are broadly confined to the northern half of the European continent and the countries of emigration, with the single exception of Ireland, to the south – Belgium, France, the German Federal Republic, Luxembourg, the Netherlands, Sweden, Switzerland and the United Kingdom

---

1 G. Beijer, Modern patterns of international migratory movements, in J. A. Jackson, ed., *Migration*, Cambridge, 1969, p.p. 11–59.

are today the main countries recruiting foreign labour while those sending labour are principally those countries along the Mediterranean coast with a large proportion of the population still employed in agriculture and a relatively low degree of industrial development. The 1965 figures based on estimates from various sources used by Rose usefully suggest the contrast between these two groups of countries in terms of manpower needs and development.

Table 1

Percentages of Occupied Manpower in Agriculture[2]

A Countries	%	B Countries	%
Belgium	6	Greece	55
France	18	Ireland	32
Germany (Fed. Republic)	11	Italy	26
Luxembourg	14	Portugal	42
Netherlands	10	Spain	35
Sweden	12	Turkey	75
Switzerland	9	Yugoslavia	57
United Kingdom	4		

This internal movement between the industrially under-developed and developed countries of Europe has of course been matched by continuing regional redistribution within the various countries. Recruitment from rural areas has, however, been generally insufficient to meet labour demands in the immigration countries. Consequently they have increasingly come to depend on the availability of a pool of foreign workers. These workers in turn have been attracted by the improved wages and living standard available in the immigration countries when compared with their own.

In these basic characteristics the features of the familiar "pull-push" model clearly operate so far as both the incentive for the immigration country with its need for labour resources, particularly unskilled labour and the attractions for the migrant to move from a relatively deproved situation to one of relative affluence. If we are to explore the significance of this migratory process within the framework of patterns of social change in Europe as a whole, however, it is necessary to consider the various national policies which serve to inhibit the operation of a free labour market in Europe. It is these differences in underlying attitude which demonstrate the reaction of the various countries to the pressures for migration and lead at one extreme to the continued willingness of certain countries to continue to take in migrants no longer essential to their rationalized manpower structures and at the other the refusal of certain countries, notably in Eastern Europe, to permit emigration even where there is a labour surplus.

2 Adapted from A. M. Rose, *Migrants in Europe; problems of acceptance and adjustment*, The University of Minnesota Press, Minneapolis, 1969, p. 12.

This paper is not intended to replicate the increasingly detailed and adequate summaries of European migration data that are now available;[3] rather it will concentrate on the result of this pattern of post-war migration on the structure of European populations and in particular the reactions of the host societies to the realities of pluralism. The reaction of the immigration country to foreign labour may be considered as a variable indicating receptivity to pluralism irrespective of the actual extent of immigration which takes place. Indeed one may find that countries with high proportions of foreign workers exhibit more xenophobia in their attitudes and consequently limit the extent to which the migrants are treated at parity with nationals in the receiving country.

Rose uses openness of the host society as a key variable in his extensive analysis of the acceptance of foreigners in European countries. The main conclusion of his excellent and informative study of legislation, attitudes and the indicators of accommodation and adjustment in the various countries is that: "What *is* important for integration and adjustment is the openness of the *immigrant* country – certainly in its overt policies, programs and practices, and probably in its informal attitudes as well."[4] In this paper an attempt will be made to develop this point in relation to the effect of migration within the European framework where the discussion of migration has begun to assume a far more mature style. Some of the shrouds of nationalism are being replaced by a riper understanding of the total process of human mobility and the widening possibilities of multi-lateral relationships between citizens and states.

It is only a few years since, in Britain, the *cri de coeur* in response to the "Brain Drain" of scientists and doctors emigrating to the United States was expressed in terms of "they owe it to the country which reared and trained them". The nation, nationality, citizenship and social identity have been held to be coterminous with personal identity and personal economic necessity. The myth of the static state has once again been strongly imposed on European thinking whatever the dynamic realities of post-war development and change. In terms of such a conception it is hardly a cause for surprise that national policies regarding immigrant workers have at best welcomed them as a painful necessity or a temporary expedient and at worst disenfranchised them and abused their civil rights by allowing the development of immigrant ghettoes. The spectrum of national attitudes toward immigrants in Western Europe suggest the emergence of policies by default rather than design; consequently emigrants are seen principally as a "bad riddance" or "failures of the system" while immigrants experience a variety of official responses, few of them allowing full and equivalent status with the native born.

The conceptual problems underlining contemporary migration policies are

---

3 See for instance: *International Migration of Manpower: Bibliography*, OECD, Paris, 1969; R. Descloîtres, *The Foreign Worker; adaptation to industrial work and urban life*, OECD, Paris, 1967; A. M. Rose, *Migrants in Europe*, op. cit.; G. Beijer, Modern International Migratory Movements, in J. A. Jackson, ed., *Migration*, Cambridge, 1969, pp. 11–59.

4 Op. cit., A. M. Rose, *Migrants in Europe*, p. 149.

rooted in a necessary rethinking of manpower policy and national autonomy on the part of major European nations. It is symptomatic of the situation where domestic national issues have such an overwhelming place in official thinking that the section of the recent review of manpower policy in the United Kingdom defines the major problems for manpower policy as follows:

> "In the long term: How can employment opportunities be steered to the areas of chronic labour surplus, thus reducing unemployment and promoting the expansion of internally competing industries? How can the necessary supply of skilled labour, hitherto notoriously scare, be secured for those areas and sectors where it will be able to make the optimal contribution? How can rigidities and resistance to technological change be overcome and a better utilisation of all manpower resources at the place of work be promoted?
> In the short term: During an anti-inflationary action by overall fiscal-monetary means, how can the tendencies towards increased unemployment be neutralised, particularly for the most vulnerable groups and sensitive areas? How can the "shake-out" be led to result in a positive "redeployment" as soon as possible? How can those who, in spite of positive counter-measures, become exposed to redundancy and unemployment be compensated in an equitable way so as to avoid human suffering and social unrest during the transitional period?
> Questions for both short- and long-term: How should local and sectoral disturbances of an inflationary or depressive nature be countered rapidly, before they develop into major imbalances needing such big and drastic corrections that considerable negative side effects are inevitable? How, when the labour market is in sustainable balance, can meaningful employment be given even to those marginal groups which have previously been mobilised only during periods of general and acute shortage of labour?"[5]

It will be noted that migrant labour is not once mentioned and yet Britain depends heavily on immigrant labour for some essential sectors of the economy and has been one of the main countries of immigration since the end of the war.

This example characterises the generally low level of consideration which the migrant receives from government and official policy. Part, at least, of the benefit of the immigrant for the receiving country has consisted of spare labour capacity to balance those areas in which there is a shortfall of labour need. National policy tends here to reflect that of employers – the chief attraction of foreign labour remains that it is in some sense "cheap labour". This is especially notable in the extent to which foreign workers are recruited to do the, mainly, unskilled work which local labour is no longer willing to perform.

It is an inevitable consequence of this that in some sense or another foreign workers tend to be subject to disparities in treatment with nationals – by default in provisions, neglect in regulations or merely the operation of local protectionist influences. Irrespective of social and personal costs involved in the process of migration itself, the fact of extensive voluntary migration has had important and positive effects on European society.

However, the process of assimilation and acceptance of the immigrant populations in Europe has been substantially inhibited by the lack of a definite policy toward immigrants or a programme designed specifically to assist and develop their association into the new society. Migrants from the Mediter-

---

5 *Manpower Policy in the United Kingdom*, OECD, Paris, 1970, p. 14.

ranean countries working in Germany or France, Irish immigrants to Britain, and so on, have not merely been employed as casual workers but have usually been encouraged by formal or informal procedures to think of their stay in the receiving country as relatively short-term. For the most part they are temporary migrants expecting to return to their homeland and, in the event of a recession or under conditions where the host country will not renew their permits, being expected to return. These initial attitudes however bear little relation to the real case. The extent of repatriation is relatively small a proportion of the total immigrant population. Of a total of 2,308,000 Italian residents in Belgium, France, Germany, Luxembourg, Netherlands, Switzerland and the United Kingdom in 1964 only 174,210 (7.54%) returned to their home land.[6]

The attitude towards repatriation varies between the different receiving countries but only France, Belgium and Sweden have a definite policy encouraging the integration of a major part of the immigrant population. Britain has been moving toward such a policy in recent years and permits permanent residence and encourages parity of treatment with other nationals. Such parity is very largely enjoyed by her "concealed" minority of nearly a million Irishborn who are affected neither by the provisions applying to aliens nor those specifically concerned with Commonwealth immigrants.

The Irish enjoy a structural relationship with Britain which makes provision, informally, for the fact of extensive and continuing migration, even though few positive arrangements exist to facilitate the process or assist the migrant. However, it is an informative case which is worth developing fairly freely because it raises issues which have a broader significance in the rest of Europe.

Following the "Easter Rising" of 1916, the 26 counties of the present Irish Republic moved toward a gradual independence from Britain. The civil war of 1921–22 gave way to a formally established Irish Free State in which Britain still retained various interests, such as naval ports, where there was a great deal of British investment and where many British citizens (identifying with Britain) continued to reside in Ireland. The Treaty which granted independence to Ireland was inclusive rather than exclusive in its arrangements for citizens and made tacit recognition of the continuing realities of a situation where heavy emigration on the Irish side, and economic interests on the other defined a practical situation in which a high degree of overlap between the two nations continued.

A good example of how this worked in practice is suggested by the Second World War during which Britain recruited an extensive amount of labour from Ireland in spite of the fact that Ireland retained a neutral status throughout the war. This did not prevent a very large number of Irish residents from wishing to help in the British war effort, or at least find work in Britain, quite apart from the considerable number who served in the British armed forces, just as many continue to do today.

---

6 Op. cit., A. M. Rose, *Migrants in Eurpe*, p. 137.

In the course of this period a close working liaison was established by the British Ministry of Labour on the one hand, who appointed a permanent official in Dublin specifically to handle applications from workers, and the Irish government. The relationship between the two countries during the war was not always easy since the emphatic neutrality of the Irish Republic clashed with the wartime needs of the British. These difficulties were largely surmounted including the difficult question of whether Irish workers living in Britain would be subject to enlistment in the British military forces. The British position was clarified in a statement which appeared in the International Labour Review in September 1943:

> "The liability of Irish workers to be called up under the British National Service Acts depends upon the question of Domicile. It is held that workers who have come from Ireland for war work since the outbreak of war and who intend to return there not later than the end of the war are resident in Great Britain for a temporary purpose only and so are not liable to be called up. They are, however, subject in the same way as British workers to other regulations."[7]

The pragmatic and *ad hoc* arrangements made during the war, though now only of historical interest, have tended to characterise a series of similar facilitating arrangements between government departments which stop short of migration policy in any particular sense. These specific wartime arrangements are interesting because they demonstrate the broad thesis that the structural arrangement affecting migrants tends to be defined *primarily* in terms of the self-interest of national governments or other parties affected by the migration rather than the needs, aspirations and interests of the migrants themselves. Consequently administrative needs such as those affecting taxation, social security, unemployment and pension benefits tend to bring together governments whose citizens are participating in either permanent or temporary migration. If, as in the Irish case, there are no controls on entry or exit these administrative arrangements tend to become more complex and inclusive of the immigrant and to differentiate him less in legal and administrative terms form the native-born.

The broad principle is expressed by the reciprocal Insurance agreements established between the United Kingdom and Ireland whereby:

> "An insured person who moves from one country to another, except those temporarily away or on government service of the originating country, is entitled to have his insurance transferred if he claims benefits. Such benefits are payable only at the Irish rate, in the case of Irish emigrants until they have made a minimum of thirteen contributions in Britain".
> "Similar arrangements exist for Maternity Allowance, Maternity Grant and Unemployment Benefit. *Dependants in one country can be counted in the other when assessing benefits.* This also applies to taxation allowances.[8]

---

7 The Transfer of Irsh workers to Great Britain, *International Labour Review*, Vol. XLVIII, No. 3, September 1943, p. 342. On the general wartime situation see Ministry of Labour, *Report of the Years 1939–1946*, London, 1947, especially pp. 188–199.
8 (My italics) J. A. Jackson, Ireland, in *Emigrant Workers Returning to their home country*, *Supplement to the Final Report*, OECD, Paris, 1967, p. 118.

As agreements for free labour movement have been achieved in Europe they have exhibited similar characteristics and have depended on the development of consequential administrative links between the respective government and administrative departments in the various countries. The process of establishing such links is, of course, greatly facilitated where close economic ties already exist and where a broadly similar taxation structure and monetary policy operates.

The Scandinavian Common Labour Market which was established (as the Nordic Labour Zone) in 1954 provided for free internal mobility on the basis of an identity card issued by one of the four countries – Denmark, Norway, Sweden, Finland. A similar agreement was reached for the three Benelux countries and the gradualist arrangements begun in 1961 and concluded in 1969 have provided for similarly free labour mobility within the six Common Market countries. Although by no means uniform the broad aim of these measures has been to produce a situation where whenever a foreign worker is admitted for employment he can enjoy identical status with indigenous workers. Although much progress has been made in support of this principle actual practice has varied widely for reasons which we shall discuss further below. Nevertheless governments, including those outside these European groupings, have made unilateral treaties for similar broad purposes. The overall result has been to provide a broad superstructure which limits some of the costs of migration to the migrant. Nevertheless a number of basic problems still remain virtually untouched by these measures and there are still wide discrepancies of policy toward foreign workers governed by specific national considerations. It also must be noted that migration between the relatively advanced European countries covered by these comprehensive agreements is only a small part of the total migration process. They can, in any case, go only a little way toward solving the more fundamental differences between immigrant and host community – thus an O.E.C.D. report:

> "...only about 15 per cent (of the 7–8 million foreign workers in Western Europe) speak the same language, and more than half speak a tongue which belongs to a completely different linguistic family. An estimated one out of three are completely illiterate, and some two-thirds come from traditional rural societies and thus have no experience of urban or industrial life. Almost a fifth are from Moslem nations, and of the immigrants from other Christian cultures, the large majority are of a different religion from the one predominant in the country to which they migrate".[9]

It is generally the case that the broad administrative arrangements concerned with unilateral or multilateral agreements between emigrant and immigrant countries do not cover the situations which arise from the day to day problems of the immigrant himself. Few countries, Italy and Spain are the exceptions here, make any serious attempt to prepare emigrants before departure and the extent to which aid is given on arrival depends very much on the ex-

---

9 Foreign Workers: a problem of social adaptation, *OECD Observer*, No. 25, Dec. 1956, pp. 11–14.

tent to which the migrant is viewed simply in terms of the needs of casual labour or as a long term investment in a "new citizen".

Two main structural variables operate in relation to the accommodation of the contemporary foreign worker in Western European societies. The first is the length of stay in the receiving country and the second is the desire on the part of that country to accept the newcomer as more than a temporary worker. The length of stay is governed by official policies affecting both the worker and his dependant relatives. Where there is a policy promoting acceptance of the immigrant as potentially a permanent addition to the national population there tend to be no limits on length of stay and encouragement for relatives to also enter the country. Such is the case, for instance, in Sweden which has reciprocal agreements with Yugoslavia, and in France. In contrast there is no encouragement for migrants to be admitted to Switzerland except on a very temporary basis. Similarly the application of these procedures varies. While technically foreign visitors need a work permit and otherwise can only be admitted to the country as tourists nearly every European country with the exception of the United Kingdom and Switzerland allows visitors to get a job and then apply for a permit.[10] In France the casual entry which is later "regularised" is the usual formula which is employed in relation to immigrants and accounts in part for the relative ease with which "illegal emigrants" from Portugal can enter France and obtain work.[11]

Just as policies vary with regard to the admission of migrant workers so there are also different policies toward admitting their families. Those countries which admit families freely usually have specific bilateral agreements. Belgium, for instance, has treaties with Turkey, Spain and Greece and will make substantial grants toward travel costs if the worker has found accommodation.[12] France, Germany, Luxembourg, Sweden, and the United Kingdom have made it relatively easy, or encouraged workers to bring families with them or subsequently. The Netherlands has liberalized a policy which until 1964 tended to oppose the entry of families of foreign workers; Germany imposes strict standards and in practical terms discourages workers from bringing their families, while Switzerland does not usually admit families, which is consistent with a general policy of admitting foreign labour on a temporary basis only. Here again there are specific exceptions.

The official policies governing length of stay and encouragement to stay permanently are reflected in a complexity of specific and selective measures governing the status of aliens. Although the specific bilateral agreements and the wider E.E.C. and other provisions for labour mobility provide a framework

---

10   Op. cit., A. M. Rose, *Migrants in Europe*. This practice was varied in 1966–67 in response to economic recession in the receiving country.

11   For a discussion of Portugal and Portugese migrants see an unpublished diploma monograph by M. Poinard, Les Portugais dans la region Rhone-Alps (Faculty of Arts, University of Lyons).

12   The grant is 50% if there are more than three children. See op. cit., A. M. Rose, *Migrants in Europe*, p. 81.

for the rationalization of policy between certain countries a great variety of policies exist and many immigrants to European countries are unaffected by such agreements and are subject to quite distinct immigration policies operated in terms of specific national interests. The Commonwealth Immigration Acts in Britain represent only one example of a policy developed in terms of specific obligations to a colonial population with nominal British nationality which is reflected in measures that are quite distinct from those affecting either immigrants from Ireland or non-British workers wishing to enter the country from European countries.

The policies that we have so far considered in a necessarily general survey have been based primarily on consideration of manpower needs and employment prospects. The concern of national governments has been directed toward facilitating labour mobility so as to meet labour needs and it has only been later that they have been forced to take note of some of the consequential problems associated with migration. As the number of immigrant workers has increased there has developed both a functional clustering in specific sectors of employment (often as a direct result of official recruitment policies) and a locational clustering which has led to the creation of immigrant communities assuming in some cases a ghetto-like structure in relation to the indigenous population. Although in few countries, other than Switzerland, do the immigrants represent more than some five per cent of the population, they are unevenly distributed so as to create large concentrations of foreign workers in certain districts and in certain industries. This causes an exaggeration of all of the problems connected with adaptation and absorption of the immigrants into the host society; problems already apparent in the range of differences which characterise the two populations.

These social and cultural differences have been summarised excellently by Descloitres[13] and I shall only note a few of them here. The vast majority of immigrants come from rural areas whether they be Irish in Britain, Algerians in France, Southern Italians in Germany, Anatolian Turks in Belgium. They migrate to primarily urban areas, or areas of urban growth in Western Europe and this emphasises a range of disparities associated with the rural-urban contrast. The broadly ascriptive qualities characteristic of the emigration areas are contrasted with the achievement emphasis of the urban areas and are indicated by the high illiteracy rates found among the immigrants and relatively low levels of educational attainment.[14] These contrasts are not a new phenomenon in migration experience and apply even to internal movements from rural to urban areas within the same country. However, they are greatly emphasised where, as in France or Britain or Germany, a large proportion of immigrants are drawn from countries which have broad cultural dissimilarities in addition. As Descloitres has put it in conjunction with his expectation that the

---

13   Op. cit., R. Descloîtres, The Foreign Worker, OECD, Paris, 1967, p. 60.
14   See for instance *Measures of adjustment of rural manpower to industrial work and urban areas*, OECD, Paris, 1968, and *Emigrant Workers returning to their home country, Final Report*, OECD, Paris, 1967.

number of immigrants from the cultural areas outside Europe must be expected
to rise substantially in the future:

> "...those immigrants who hail from the Mediterranean Moslem societies and the trans-
> continental cultural areas occupy the lowest, if not completely marginal, positions in
> European societies. All possible factors conspire to bring this about: almost total "other-
> ness", ignorance, the awful over-simplification of concepts ensuring therefrom, the strength
> of prejudices aroused by their more overt characteristics (colour, strongly marked ethnic
> traits), the seeming outlandishness of their practices and behaviour which is merely
> aggravated by repetition, etc. Even if these impediments to social integration were over-
> come there would still remain linguistic ignorance or chonic unintelligibility due to incur-
> able habits of stress and accent, frequent instances of illiteracy, and lack of vocational
> training in the majority of cases."[15]

These immigrants from Africa, Asia, the West Indies and Turkey represent
perhaps a quarter of the total immigrant population in Western Europe but
they exhibit in an extreme form the characteristic problems of immigrant acceptance within a host population which affect most European countries today
in one form or another. The emphasis on manpower needs as distinct from
long term considerations of adaptation that has characterised official policy,
on short term interests rather than long term and on the migrant worker as a
"stop-gap" in a period of industrial expansion, has too often tended to under-
estimate the social and demographic consequences of these policies within
European countries.

   Whether the immigrant stays a long or a short time depends partly on official attitudes, labour permits, the availability of employment in different sectors, and the operation of social security and other administrative machinery.
The attitude toward relatives is clearly another significant variable. It is open
to a country to encourage its emigrants, or a selected group of them, to stay
permanently or to return fairly swiftly to their country of origin. Rose has demonstrated moderate significance in his hypothesis relating the openness of
the policies of the host society to the adaptation of its immigrants[16] Thus countries like France may adopt a deliberate policy of "Francification" with some
success, especially when, as in the Gaullist period, it was associated with a clear-
cut nationalism and a policy of expansion. Other countries, such as Switzerland,
may enforce a policy of short stay permits in order not to upset the delicate
political and social balance of the Swiss Cantons by giving migrants full and
equivalent status with the indigenous population.

   Such attitudes among the citizens and governments of the receiving countries are matched by corresponding attitudes on the part of immigrants themselves. The large majority view their stay as temporary initially but gradually
as they establish a niche for themselves in the new society the advantages of
return become less evident and this is particularly the case when families are
permitted to come with or join the migrant worker. However in terms of the
migration process the emigrants interests are short term – he puts up with

---

15 Op. cit., R. Descloîtres, *The Foreign Worker*, p. 64.
16 Op. cit., A. M. Rose, *Migrants in Europe*, pp. 147 ff.

conditions of work, of housing and of intolerance which are only endurable because he does not expect them to last too long. Such short term orientations inevitably serve further to limit aspiration for training, for advancement, responsibility or promotion at work, for the attainment of skills or the accumulation of capital. Generally high earnings (because overtime is an important incentive) are sent home as remittances to be spent supporting the largely economically weak institutions from which the migrant has come.

The shift to a long-term perspective is accidental and gradual for the most part, and lacking aspirations for achievement the migrant tends in any case to be denied equal opportunities in practice – either because he does not know the language, the local customs, or the conventions of the local society, or because he is excluded in practice from avenues of participation available to the 'host' population. Given the subtle and subjective characteristics of discrimination it would be surprising if the immigrant were to be actively assisted to those advantages to which he may be entitled. Lack of preparation at home, lack of official guidance and policy in the receiving country both combine to make the process liable to chance circumstances.

In such a situation even the best intentioned policy does not preclude extensive practical disparity of treatment between immigrants and indigenous workers. The practical operation of a manpower policy tends toward a resistance on the part of employers and foreign workers to take advantages of possibilities for training or advancement. On the part of the employers purely rational criteria such as the need for unskilled labour tend to define the role of the foreign worker; from the worker's point of view the job is a means of achieving short term interests defined by an orientation to the country of origin. As Allefrede has written "their dream is not integration into our society but a higher status in their own ... the basic problem of temporary immigrants is to *adapt temporarily* to a community where they are mainly in transit; they do not try to assimilate at all costs nor do they complain when opportunities or assimilation are not offered."[17]

In practice of course discrimination against migrants is a good deal more positive than this and the areas where there are large concentrations of immigrant nationals exhibit a degree of discrimination and prejudice toward the newcomers which tends to be sharply exacerbated in the event of economic recession. The areas with heavy recent concentrations of migrant workers such as the Birmingham concentration in the United Kingdom, the Lyons region in France and Cologne in West Germany, exhibit these tendencies with approximately 10% of the active labour force drawn from outside the country.

There is little indication in practice that this post-war migration into Europe and between European countries has achieved any extensive development toward integration or Europeanization. The extent of assimilation with the host population is in general very slight and is likely to remain so until at

---

17 M. Allefrede from a discussion paper on the Form and Effects of Foreign Immigration in the Lyons region, 1969, unpublished.

least the second generation (the children of the present migrants) reach maturity. In spite of the difficulties that have been outlined here the post-war migration within Western Europe has been a remarkably successful process in social as well as economic terms. Though it may not, of itself, have achieved any elimination of the nationalist orientation that has tended to characterise migration policy it has provided for the development of a set of procedures which protect the emigrant and in some cases actively encourage him not merely as a source of labour but as an active participant in the host society.

The decade 1959–1969 was a period of particularly heavy movement within Europe of migrant workers. West Germany, for instance, in the two year period 1959–1960 had a net immigration of over 500 thousand, while France partly as a result of the repatriation of population from North Africa had a net immigration of 1,430 thousand in the four years 1960–63. Immigration into the United Kingdom was already past its peak in this period but in the period between 1958 and 1963 (mid year) there was a net immigration of 443 thousand. In these countries the significance of migration can be expressed by taking net immigration as a percentage of natural increase. This shows that immigration accounts for one-fifth of the population increase in the United Kingdom, over a half in Germany and for this specific period a considerably greater proportion in France.[18]

The demographic significance of these migrations depends in part on the policy of the receiving country in relation to the family of the immigrant. The encouragement of immigrants' relatives may ease the process of migration and be less disruptive for the individual migrant. On the other hand it may operate against a process of full integration with the host populations. In any case it is a question to which different considerations apply when it is asked of the young unmarried or the older immigrant with wife and children.

Beijer has summed up these questions in his statement that "the greatest social benefit of international voluntary migration, though there are also social costs, is the opportunity to reduce narrow nationalism in Europe and other parts of the world."[19] It is a potent and challenging dream. However, migration will not of itself serve to produce more than raw material for a process of acceptance and absorption with as great a potential for divisiveness as for unity. The process is essentially dynamic and capable of development in a number of alternative ways. We must now assume that the romantic ideal of complete assimilation within one or two generations is just as unreal as the total rejection of immigrant absorption called for by some members of the indigenous populations. Plurality suggests an alternative which enables even if it does not ensure the immigrants' position to be sustained in the society to which he comes without undue disadvantage and hardship.

The assumptions underlying the notion of plural society in Europe do not

---

18 *Demographic Trends: 1965–1980 in Western Europe and North America*, OECD, Paris, 1966, p. 13.
19 G. Beijer, Modern patterns of International migratory movements, in J. A. Jackson (ed.), *Migration*, Cambridge, 1969, p. 59.

rest on a notion of an homogenized European society. Rather they recognise diversity and welcome the potential contribution and enrichment to be derived from it. Such an acceptance does not conflict with the maintenance of distinctive national and regional identities – rather it encourages them within a context which secures a common ground of agreed principles and recognition of equal rights which can allow such diversity to flourish. Too often in the past the position of minority populations has been exacerbated by formal and informal mechanisms which introduce continuing structural determinants of their disadvantaged position. There are sufficient examples of this tendency today in Birmingham, Lyons or Cologne. Nevertheless one can be optimistic that the climate of opinion generally in the European countries is free of those extremes of xenophobia which develop ideological barriers to fortify the quite sufficient practical difficulties surrounding the migration process.

Marriage-Rates in Sweden

JAN TROST

Uppsala

THE marriage-rate and changes in the marriage-rate are of importance in several connections, e.g. in planning administrative organizations that are directly or indirectly affected by it. Since there normally is a cultural and empirical correlation between the marriage-rate and fertility etc., changes in the marriage-rate can be seen as an index of, or reflecting, other social and societal changes.

We shall here look at the marriage-rate in Sweden during the last two decades and try to find explanations for the changes that have occurred.

As can be seen from the dotted line in figure 1, the marriage-intensity of men, measured in numbers of marriages in relation to numbers of un-married men, decreased slowly from 1950 until 1964, in which year it started to increase slightly. But since 1967 it has decreased markedly. The tendency is the same for women (figure 2). In order to reach a more detailed picture and to try to provide an "explanation" of the tendencies, the marriage-rates for different age-brackets are calculated and presented in the same figures.

From these we can conclude that in the higher-age brackets (over 35 years) there were, during the two decades under discussion, slow, steady decreases, but in the lower age groups the decrease during the last three years is remarkable.

From figure 1 we can see that for men 25–29 years of age, there has been an enormous increase from about 140 per mille in 1950, to more than 200 in 1964, and then a larger decrease back to 146 in 1969. The tendency is the same for the lower-age bracket, for which the change in the marriage-rate is just about as big as for the 25–29 group (it is, of course, open to discussion whether a change from 140 to 210 is about the same as, or much more than, from 75 to 105; however, this will not be discussed here).

Regardless of age, the marriage-rate for men has decreased from 52 per mille to 40, but it is only for ages of over 30 that the age-specific rates decrease totally the two decades. A relevant piece of information here is that in only about 20 per cent of the marriages the men are older than 30 years.

The figures for women differ from those for the men. We find (figure 2) that the marriage-rate independent of age decreases during the two decades from 48 per mille to 38, but the age-specific data show a different picture for women than for men. In all age-brackets the rate is higher in 1950 than in 1969. Thus, the rate for the age-bracket 15–19 goes from 33 per mille to 16; for the bracket 20–24 from 170 to 144; for the bracket 25–29 from 170 to 155; for the bracket 30–34 from 105 to 74, and for the bracket 35–39 from 58 to 38 per mille.

We find the same phenomenon as for men; a rapid decrease during the last few years for lower ages.

Since it might be reasonable to argue that the tendencies in first marriages could be different from those in later marriages, there figures have also been calculated. From figure 3 we see that the tendencies are exactly the same for all marriages. From figure 4 we observe that the same is true for women. This is what we could expect, because about 90% of all marriages are first marriages for men; the corresponding figure for women is only slightly higher.

There are two things that need explanation as far as we can see:

a) the increase in marriage-intensity in the period from 1950 to the middle of the sixties, and
b) the rapid decrease since the middle of the sixties.

a) The increase: 1950–1966

To repeat: the increase for men in the overall figures is only noticeable in the lower age-brackets – i.e. below 35 years – whereas in the higher brackets there is a decrease. For women the increase is noticeable only in the ages of 20–29; for higher ages the rate is either constant or decreases. Davis (1956, p. 243) assumes that "the personal outlook of masses of individuals is affected... by economic and political conditions", which in this context means that if the conditions are bad, marriages are postponed and if the conditions are good the marriage-rate will increase. This assumption can be used as an explanation of the increase in the marriage-rates in Sweden during the fifties and the first half of the sixties. There is no doubt that the living-conditions in particular were good. Wages increased and the standard of living rose steadily; no serious economic or political crisis occurred. However, the conditions did not improve rapidly, which can be indicated by the constant, or slowly increasing marriage-rates. In passing it can be noted that the divorce-rate in Sweden was almost constant during the same period (Trost, 1970).

Swedish society has had a policy of making available to young families several kinds of financial assistance, e.g. better loans for establishing new homes, financial subsidies for the family when the husband/father is doing his obligatory duty in the army, increased subsidies for children under 16 years, more kindergartens, etc. All these programmes mentioned and others not here mentioned contribute towards making it easier for young families, especially those with children – which is the normal situation for young families (of below).

As an explanation of the decreased marriage-rate we shall point out the unpopularity of marriage as a legal state below, but it does not seem reasonable to use the same argument here in a reversed way, because there are no known tendencies showing that legal marriage should have become more and more popular as such (of below). Since Carlsson (1970) has made an analysis of data from 1930 to 1965 concerning "internal" relations it seems superfluous to go into details here. So we limit the analysis to the above discussed possible causes or "external" relations.

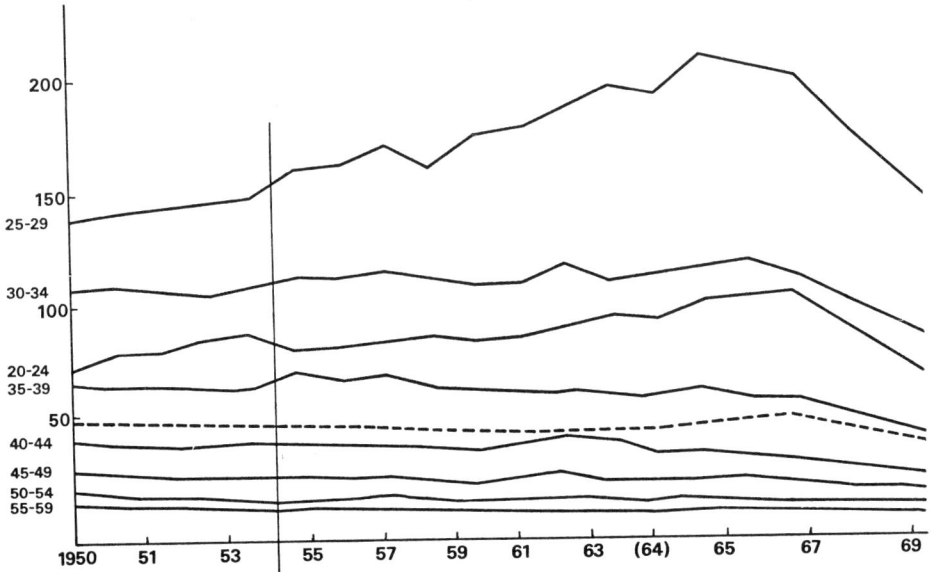

Fig. 1. Males, marriages per 1,000 not-married.

b) The decrease: after 1966

Our interest lies more in the problems and attempts to explain the decrease in the marriage-rate during the last years of the sixties. As we found from figures

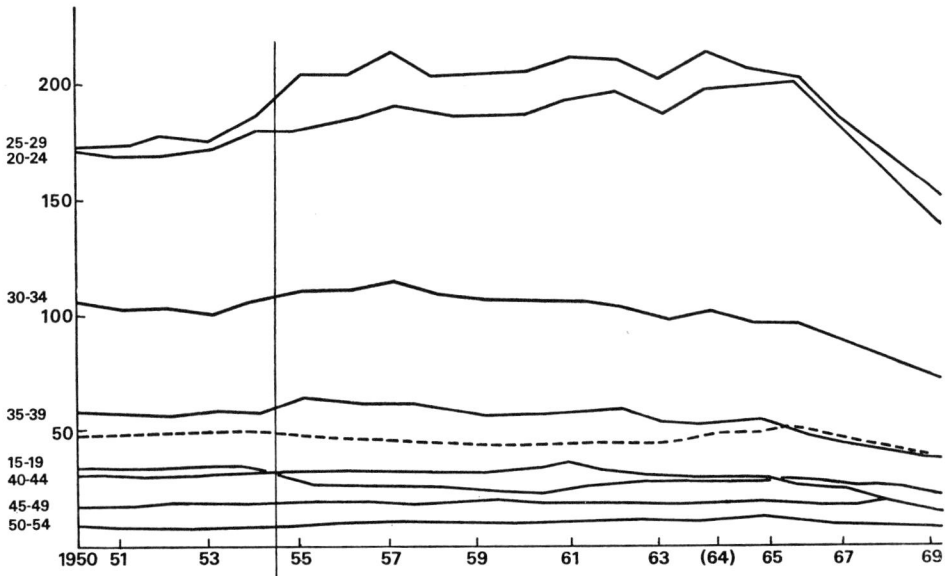

Fig. 2. Females, marriages per 1,000 not-married.

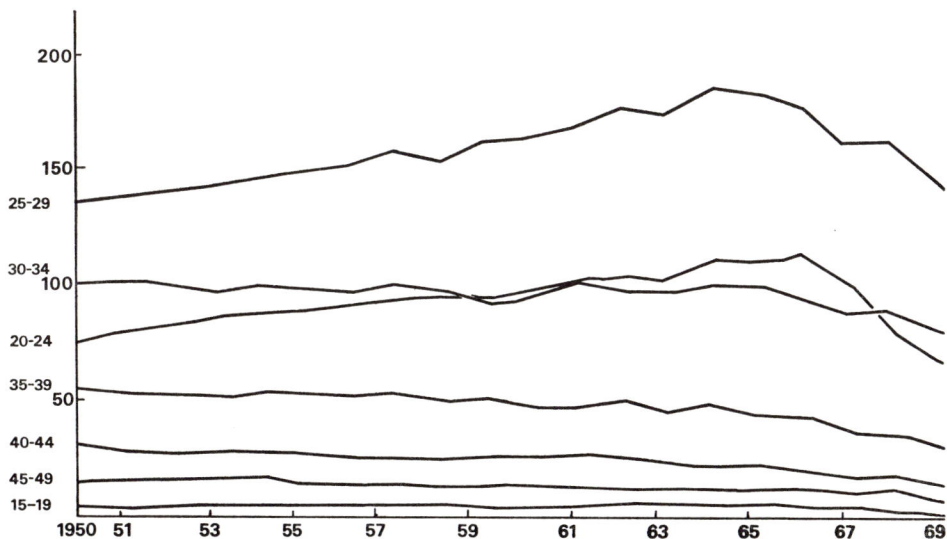

Fig. 3. Males, married in first marriage per 1,000 not-married.

1–4, there are remarkable decreases in the marriage-rate, especially in the lower-age brackets irrespective of sex and irrespective of whether the calculation is based on all marriages or based only on first marriages. This decrease started in 1967 and went on steadily through 1968 and 1969.

This decrease might just be a sudden and temporary one, which implies that in a few years an increase will occur so that the level of the middle of the

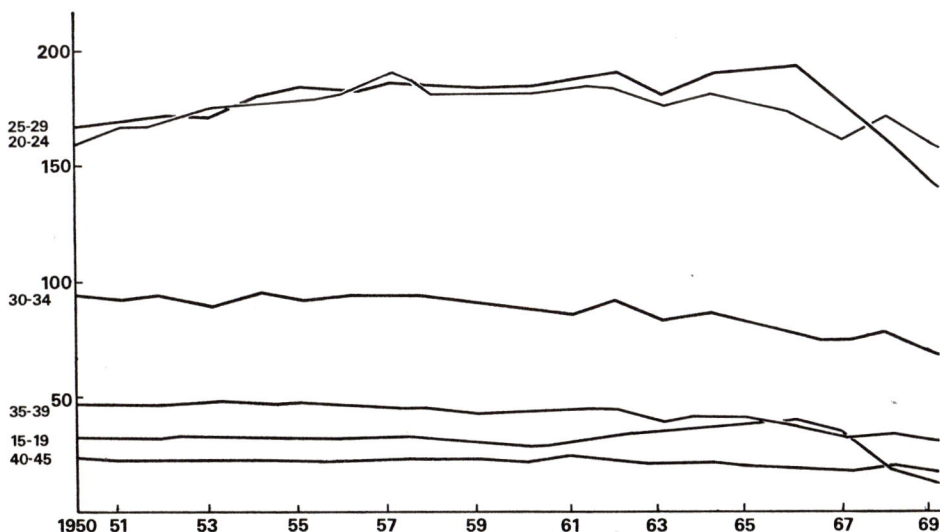

Fig. 4. Females, married in first marriage per 1,000 not-married.

sixties will be reached again. However, it is important to note that the overall marriage-rate and the marriage-rates for almost all age-brackets of 1969 are lower than the rates of 1950. As shown by Carlsson (1970), there has been a slow, steady increase since 1930. From this it follows that the rate in 1950, which is the first year of this present study, was, in a modern-historical sense, relatively high and that the rate in 1966 – the peak year – was very high; high, that is, in relation to Swedish culture, which according to Hajnal (1956) has a relatively low nuptiality.

Davis (1956, p. 255) says that marriage has "become much more respon-sive to current conditions, almost like the swings of fashion". But a fashion can become stable, which means that fashion is not a transitory thing, but has a long duration. Evidently, Davis (1956, p. 245) does not believe in this in con-nection with the marriages, since he says that the changes in marriage-rate "from one year to another do not represent lifetime decisions to enter, or stay permanently out of, wedlock, but rather decisions as to the particular time of marriage". He calls this phenomenon "postponed" or "borrowing on the fu-ture". If this supposition is correct, a decline of the marriage-rate like that in Sweden during the last three years will in a very few years be followed by an increase that will be about rapid as the decrease has been.

It seems as if Davis talks only on a cohort level in the sense that a number of individuals follow a modern line of thoughts or idea just for a while – that is to say that they postpone their marriages. But it could be true that these in-dividuals would remain unmarried (by unmarried is meant all those that are not married i.e. even divorced, widowed) in spite of the fact that they behaved in accordance with a fashion; some people who are radical in that they readily adopt new ideas quite quickly grow conservative in the same sense that they stick to the adopted idea whatever may happen. If this last line thought is correct and if it is the fashion not to marry, then marriage-rate in Sweden will in a few years increase again, but slowly.

One kind of data that is in line with Davis' idea of a "fashion" on an indi-vidual and an occasional level is the trend in the number of "pregnancy marria-ges". (By pregnancy marriage is meant a marriage where the wife has given birth to a legitimate child within six months after the wedding.) From table 1, column 11, we perceive that the relative number of pregnancy marriages de-creased markedly during the last three years (1967–1969) as did the marriage-rate. This fact is irrespective of which of the two measures offered (in table 1) we use – number of pregnancy marriages in relation to the total number of live births or the number of pregnancy marriages in relation to the total number of marriages.

The reason why "fashion" is put in quotation marks in the preceeding paragraph is that the most probable explanation of the change presented can-not be considered to have anything to do with fashion. The reason why it is common to use the term "pregnancy" marriages is the assumption that in most cases, or at least with a considerable number of them, the fact that the girl has become pregnant is a stimulus for the couple to marry – in some cases

Table 1

Year	Live births	Live births out of wedlock	Legal live births	Live births 6 months after marriage	Marriages	Not-married women 15–44 years
1	2	3	4	5	6	7
1963	113′	14,172	98,731	16,438	53,480	560′
1964	123′	16,117	106,547	18,339	58,439	566′
1965	123′	16,950	105,856	18,398	59,963	568′
1966	123′	17,962	105,392	17,918	61,101	563′
1967	121′	18,323	103,037	16,063	56,561	559′
1968	113′	17,891	95,196	13,340	52,016	562′
1969	108′	17,517	90,105	11,214	48,357	576′
1970	105′					

Year	3/2 · 100	3/7 · 100	5/2 · 100	5/6 · 100	3+5/2 · 100
1	8	9	10	11	12
1963	14.4	2.53	14.5	30.7	27.1
1964	15.1	2.85	14.9	31.4	28.0
1965	16.0	2.98	15.0	30.7	28.7
1966	17.0	3.19	14.0	29.3	29.2
1967	17.8	3.28	13.3	28.4	28.4
1968	18.8	3.18	11.8	25.6	27.6
1969	19.4	3.04	10.4	23.2	26.6

Source: Data calculated from diverse published and unpublished official statistics.

they would otherwise never have married; in some other cases the couple would have postponed the wedding to a later date.

There are two main explanations for the fact that the number of pregnancy marriages has decreased. One of them has to do with preventive techniques and the other with the increase in the number of children born out of wedlock.

a) Let us consider prevention. Before 1965 the main preventive devices were condomes and diaphragms. Both of these are fairly safe if they are used, but there has to be an interruption in the foreplay to coitus if they are to be used. It is therefore reasonable that in exalted situations they are often not used. But since 1964 birth-control pills have been allowed in Sweden, which means that they came into use in 1965. Since innovations rarely cover an entire field immediately, the effects of the introduction of the pill can be assumed to have occurred in a year or so, i.e. in 1967, when the birth-rate started to decrease as shown in table 1, column 2. That the birth-control pills are commonly used in Sweden was shown by Larsson-Cohn and Trost (1970). They showed that one quarter of all females, married as well as unmarried, 15–44 years old, use birth-control pills. Taking these facts about the pill as well as the data in table 1 into consideration, it seems reasonable to assume that the use of the pill has caused the decrease in the number of live births as well of the number of pregnancy marriages. If the assumption that many of the pregnancy-marriages are "caused" by the pregnancy is correct, the increase in the use of birth-control pills has caused the decrease in the marriage-rate – especially among the lower age-brackets.

b) The second main explanation for the decrease in the number of pregnancy marriages is the increase in the number of children born out of wedlock. From table 1, column 8, we find that the number of children born out of wedlock in relation to the total number of live births has increased considerably during the last few years. This measure is, however, a crude one, since it does not take into consideration the possible producers, i.e. the unmarried women of fertile ages. But the same figure is seen in column 9, which shows the number of children born out of wedlock in relation to the number of unmarried women 15–44 years old. Thus, one could state that the decrease incidence of pregnancy marriages correlates with the increased incidence of children born out of wedlock.

But when consulting column 12 in table 1, we find that the number of children born out of wedlock *plus* the number of pregnancy marriages, in relation to the number of live births, has decreased by about ten per cent (i.e. from 29.2 to 26.6) from 1966 to 1969.

This means that the explanation in terms of pregnancy marriages is not sufficient. The increase is all the more curious since we argued that the preventive techniques have improved and have come into better or more effective use. It is therefore reasonable to assume that there has been a change in the attitude towards unmarried mothers and children born out of wedlock.

In Sweden there has been, compared to many other cultures, a positive or at least not a negative view of unmarried mothers or "illegitimate" children. But is there any reason to assume a still more "liberal" view? Or are there still other explanations?

There are some indications, which could be treated as evidence of a more "liberal" attitude; thus e.g. during the last few years more and more unmarried women announce a childbirth in the newspapers – before only married couples would do so; if there is a shortage of places in the "kindergartens" the children of unmarried mothers will be placed before other children. But at the same time the attitude toward unmarried mothers and their children has for a long time been so positive, so that it seems unreasonable to think that change of attitude could have an effect like the one indicated by table 1.

A more probable explanation seems to be the hypothesis that the number of "engagement marriages" or "conscience marriages" has increased and is effecting data shown in table 1. If the supposition that the engagement marriages have increased is valid then we have explained at least a part of the decrease in the number of marriages. It remains for us to find some justification for the hypothesis, and we have to try to establish what kind of engagement marriages there are.

But first, what is meant by the term marriage? According to the law a marriage exists when it is registered through a religious or civil act. This means of course that what has been said in this paper refers to legal marriages only and not to other stable types of dyadic formations between man and woman, which have the same function or functions as the legal marriage. What has been said earlier in this paper about the so-called engagement marriages can be considered applicable to non-legal marriages. The partners only live a marriage-way of live.

We know only that such non-legal marriages exist, but not to which extent. Polygamy is forbidden by law and there exist no or almost no polygamous non-legal marriages in Sweden. Trost (1970) pointed out that when talking about marital dyads and their formation and dissolution, it is reasonable to take four points of time into consideration (cf. figure 5).

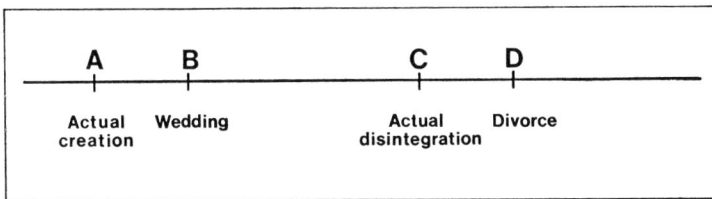

Fig. 5.

The official data do not only deal with point B, i.e. the number of weddings. From some social psychological point of view, and in relation to the suppositions made regarding engagement marriages etc., it would be very interesting to know the number of "actual creations": How many of the non-legal marriages turn into legal marriages and how long is the time-interval between points A and B? etc.: i.e. what are the numbers and nature of legal marriages and syndiasmos (a term that Löcsei (1970) introduced for functional marriages or dyads irrespective of whether they are legal marriages or not)?

Only ten years ago, people did not normally admit that they lived together in an engagement marriage. Their parents would normally have objected strongly. But since about five years ago, there has been an intensive public dialogue, for example discussions in mass media, about the old institutionalized marriage. Many speakers have expressed very negative attitudes toward legel marriage. Some have argued for free marriages, and some have argued for large families – not extended families but large families consisting of many nuclear units with neither blood nor generational acquaintanceship.

As far as yet is known the "large families" do not exist except in a very few cases, and in those few cases they have not been together for a very long time.

We do not know if the argument about the situation with no family-units at all has been or will be successful, but the third situation (non-legal marriages) is supposed to be quite common in Sweden today. In fact, nobody knows how common such marriages are, but there are some indices showing that they must be very common – clearly, we do not know either if they are more common now than some years ago.

One index showing the commonness of non-legal marriages is that which Näsholm & Näsholm (1970) found, namely that out of those that married in 1969/1970 almost 60 per cent were cohabitating before marriage. We do not know if this cohabitation has lasted for such a long time that we can state that they really had been "engagement marriages", which changed status to become legal marriages.

The study by Näsholm & Näsholm does not indicate anything about stable syndiasmos – stable in the sense of not ending in legal marriage or "separation". It seems, however, reasonable to assume that the nuclear unit is, from a social point of view, stable – i.e. it does not have to be stable in the individual case but rather in a cultural sense – as social institutions. This assumption has some similarities to the assumption by Murdock (1949) about the universality of the nuclear family. But we are not going to discuss Murdock's assumption; we only claim that our hypothesis about "engagement marriages" applies to Sweden today and for short-time periods – a culture will not change in a few years in all respects unless there is a revolution (and even a revolution is not enough, normally).

A second index of the commonness of non-legal syndiasmos is, as mentioned above, that people talk about this phenomenon very openly today, which was socially impossible ten or fifteen years ago. We do not believe that it is only what the lips say that has changed, but in fact the social reality also. On the other hand, we will not be so blind as to claim that people did *not* live together before marriage ten to fifteen years ago. But they did not live together to the same extent, with only one address, so regularly as now. Ten to fifteen years ago the social and economic situation for unmarried couples was not the same as it is today and was three years ago. The last decade can be characterized as the period when many social-welfare reforms had a great impact on Swedish society as a whole. And a great deal of this reform program has been very favourable for single individuals with children.

It seems reasonable that, if our hypothesis is correct that people postpone their marriage and live in engagement marriages for a long time instead of only having short engagements, then the age at first marriage should be higher now than a couple of years ago. We find from table 2 that this is true: the median age at first marriage has decreased by about 0.1 year per year until 1966. But for the last three years the median age at marriage (since 1966) is that especially young people postpone their marriages. This explanation is not the same as the former one, nor does it exhibit the former; it might be a specification in the sense that it deals with the younger people, while the former explanation did not separate on an age level.

A third explanation, not yet confirmed by data, is the usual declaration given especially by young people living together in "engagement marriages" that they want fo find out if they "suit" each other. This could imply the hypothesis that if they marry they will not want to divorce or even that they are

Table 2

Median age at first marriage 1950–1969

Year	Males	Females
1950	26.9	23.9
1951	26.7	23.8
1952	26.7	23.7
1953	26.6	23.6
1954	26.5	23.6
1955	26.4	23.5
1956	26.3	23.3
1957	26.2	23.2
1958	26.0	22.9
1959	25.9	22.9
1960	25.7	22.8
1961	25.4	22.6
1962	25.2	22.5
1963	25.0	22.3
1964	24.8	22.1
1965	24.6	22.1
1966	24.5	22.2
1967	24.5	22.4
1968	24.6	22.6
1969	24.8	22.7

Source: Befolkningsrörelsen, Folkmängdens Förändringar, Befolkningsförändringar, not-published official statistics.

afraid of the upsetting situation that could arise in a divorce – it is easier to "divorce" in engagement marriage than in a legal marriage. Although this view that these people are supposed to have is wrong, they act in accordance with their views – all experience shows us that it is easier if a third person (society) has set up some rules for the behaviour and the dissolution of a group than not having any predecided rules at all.

Sometimes it is supposed that engagement marriages are something new in Swedish culture – they are not. In many parts of Sweden there has been a cultured tradition that was common fifty or a hundred years ago, that couples cohabit "på tro och loven" (on vow), which means that they form a cultural but non-legal marriage. The same phenomenon still exists in Iceland, where one speaks of engagement marriages – this cultural tradition that has no correspondence in the law explains the high rate of children born out of wedlock. Culturally, though not legally, they are born in a marriage.

For a researcher on dyadic formations it is a pity that it is possibly to get data only on legal marriages, and not on other marriage – like forms, from the official statistics.

It was unfortunate earlier, but it is even more so now, since one could claim, slightly exaggerated, that it is only the emotional or primary group-

function that is left to the marital dyad in modern/welfare/society. This implies
that the now-existing law complies with the old saying of Ogburn about the
cultural lag, since the existing law affects many of the traditional family-
functions.

BIBLIOGRAPHY

Carlsson, G. (1970), *Marriages-Rates as Social Indicators*, in Scandinavian Population Studies
2, Stockholm.
Davis, K. (1956), *Statistical Perspective on Marriage and Divorce*, in Spengler, J. J. & O. T.
Duncan (eds): Demographic Analysis, Illinois.
Hajnal, J. (1956), *The Marriage Boom*, in Spengler, J. J. & O. T. Duncan (eds): Demographic
Analysis, Illinois.
Löcsli, P. (1970), *Syndiasmos in Contempory Budapest*, Budapest (mimeo).
Murdock, G. P. (1949), *Social Structure*, New York.
Näsholm, A. & Näsholm H. (1970), *Hindersprövning och olika vigselsätt* (Impediment tests and
Different Marriage Forms), Research Reports from Dept. of Sociology, Special Series, FF 8,
Uppsala.
Trost, J. (1970), *Utvecklingen i fråga om äktenskapets stabilitet* (Changes in Marital Stability),
Research Reports from Dept. of Sociology, Special Series FF 1, Uppsala.

Recent Trends of Nuptiality
in Some European Countries

A DEMOGRAPHIC ANALYSIS

Louvain

I. Introduction

THIS article is devoted to the study of the main contemporary trends of nuptiality in Europe – marriages and dissolutions of unions – examined from a purely demographic point of view. Before approaching the problem of methods of analysis and the available statistical data, it is useful to see why demographers study nuptiality[1].

The essential purpose of demography is to study the movements of human populations living in specific areas; these movements depend on only three components: natality, mortality and spatial mobility, characterized respectively by the following events, births, death and in- and out-migrations. Nuptiality is thus not a primary object of population science, as it is not an immediate component of population movement in time and space. To study population movement also implies to explain it; and by explaining natality, one of the most important components of population movement, one falls back on the study of nuptiality. In the article quoted in footnote 1, M. C. Galan, G. Machada and J. Bonmariage have put forward the following interesting *hypothesis*: by means of the study of natality, component of population movement, demographers must necessarily try to identify, in the population observed, the individuals who not only fulfill the necessary physiological conditions to procreate but who are, moreover, endowed by Society – in one way or the other – with the function of reproduction. Marriage, considered as a way of admission to procreation, becomes an important secondary variable, as it immediately acts on natality, primary component of population movement. This point of view implies, of course, that one takes into account all the socially recognized forms of marriage in *the population* observed, without considering only the legal forms of marriage. This approach can fortunately be simplified for the countries con-

---

1 See in this connection G. Wunsch, *"L'analyse de la nuptialité: un sujet de contestation"*, General Conference of the IUSSP, London 1969, and M. C. Galan-Vivas, G. N. Machado, J. Bonmariage, *"Signification démographique de la nuptialité"*, Recherches Economiques de Louvain, "Etudes démographiques", Louvain, 1969, no 4.

sidered here; in most European countries illegitimate births occurring out of *legal* marriage are not very numerous[2]. It is sufficient to consider here solely legal marriage as an institution set up by Society aiming to regulate reproduction. With this in view also the legal forms of marriage-dissolutions only will be dealt with in the following pages.

II. Methods of analysis and data collected

A rational use of data collected in Europe in the field of nuptiality implies that one first has to define the *methods of analysis* that one wishes to apply, even if one has to use, in practice, less rigorous methods if data collected do not enable one to apply the best type of analysis[3]. We shall then examine the data collected in various European countries; these data, however, are not usually *published* in an adequate form.

A. *Methods of analysis*

We will distinguish here between two different types of analysis: analysis of nuptiality from continuous registration of events[4] and population structures drawn from census statistics; analysis of nuptiality based on data collected by censuses or surveys. We shall not examine here the complex problem of analysing differential nuptiality by social categories[5]; the data *published* at the present time are inadequate for a rigorous study of this problem.

Continuous observation

With relation to *continuous registration*, in the first place, one may adopt either period analysis or cohort analysis of nuptiality. The main purpose of *period analysis* is to bring out the influence of population structures on the number of events (marriages or marriage-dissolutions) observed during a period of

---

2   The ratio of illegitimate births to the total number of births varied approximately between 2% and 10% around 1963 in European countries. See: United Nations Demographic Yearbook 1965, table 20.

3   For a more thorough study of the methods of analysis used at present in the field of nuptiality, see in particular J. Hajnal, *"Age at marriage and proportions marrying"*, Population Studies, London, November 1953; L. Henry, *"Mesure de la fréquence des divorces"*, Population, Paris, 1952, nb 2; id., *"Approximations et erreurs dans les tables de nuptialité des générations"*, Population, Paris, 1963, nb 4; A. Monnier and G. Stroobant, *"Possibilités d'analyse de la nuptialité des célibataires dans quelques pays industrialisés"*, Recherches Economiques de Louvain, 1970, nb 5; R. Pressat: *"Le remariage des veufs et des veuves"*, Population, Paris 1956, nb 1; C. Wattelar and G. Wunsch, *"Etude démographique de la nuptialité en Belgique"*, chapter I: "Les Méthodes d'analyse de la nuptialité", Department of Demography, Louvain, 1967; G. Wunsch, *"L'analyse de la nuptialité: un sujet de contestation"*, General Conference of the IUSSP, London, 1969.

4   Essentially by vital-statistics registration.

5   A theoretic design of analysis of differential nuptiality limited to the sole nuptiality of persons single is presented in the article by A. Monnier and G. Stroobant op cit.; an application of this approach is in process at the Department of Demography of the University of Louvain, using in particular data collected in Belgium and the U.S.A.

one or two years for example. Various fundamental indices can be calculated: *rates* of nuptiality obtained by dividing the number of events considered by the mean number of persons not affected by the process under study; *quotients* (probabilities) of nuptiality obtained by division of the number of events by the initial population not having experienced the process studied; finally, *reduced events* obtained by the ratio of events to the total number of individuals who have experienced the process or not. In the case of first marriage, for example, one computes a rate by dividing the number of first marriages of males or females of a given age by the mean population of bachelors or spinsters at this age; the nuptiality quotient is obtained by the ratio of first marriages to the initial number of never-married persons at a given age; finally, reduced marriages are obtained simply by dividing the number of first marriages by the mean population, married or unmarried, at a given age. These various age-specific distributions can then be summarized by the usual method of *direct* standardization[6] or, even more easily, by the sum indices. Then marriages can be classified to obtain a *crude nuptiality-rate* by dividing the total number of marriages by the total population. This ratio is frequently used but has the disadvantage of being influenced by the structure of the population; it is therefore useful to work out a measure of nuptiality obtained by the *indirect standardization* technique[7].

The methods used above can be extrapolated to marriage-dissolutions (divorce and widowhood) and to remarriages. Unfortunately, these events are most often classified by the sole *age* of the individuals. Age – specific measures of marriage-dissolution or remarriage can be obtained by dividing the events observed at a given age by the average number of individuals at this age, to eliminate the influence of the age structure of male and female populations. Ideally, data collection should also enable demographers to obtain indices eliminating the influence of marital status, or population structures according to marriage duration (for marriage-dissolutions) and the duration since marriage-dissolution (for remarriages)[8]; unfortunately, such an analysis is rarely possible, due to inadequate data collection by central statistical offices.

Still in the field of period analysis, one may use the traditional method of *synthetic cohorts* by applying period measures to a hypothetical cohort with the view to determining intensity (mean number of events per head) and tempo (mean duration of the distribution of events over time). The classical method is, in this case, to use the quotients of events with a view to setting up an *attrition table* similar to the usual life table. From this we can derive, in the case of first marriage for example, the average number of marriages per head (or its complement, the proportion ultimately single) and mean age at marriage. These

6 This method is explained in all the manuals on demography: see for example G. W. Barclay, "*Techniques of Population analysis*", John Wiley and Sons, 1958, pp. 162–166.
7 Idem.
8 See in this connection G. Wunsch, "*La théorie des événements réduits: application aux principaux phénomènes démographiques*", Recherches Economiques de Louvain, 1968, nb 4, pp. 396–400.

results are of course hypothetical; they are not applicable to any real cohort, as they are derived from period measures. Moreover they are often affected by biases which make their use critical[9].

Frequently, it is impossible to calculate an attrition table in order to derive a hypothetical intensity because of inadequate classification of data; this is especially the case in the analysis of marriage-dissolution and remarriage A palliative consists in dividing the number of events by a *weighted mean* of events characterising the various cohorts observed at a given time. In the case of divorce, for example, the number of divorces observed during a given year is divided by a weighted average of marriages which occured during the year of observation and the previous years, weights being the proportion of divorces by marriage-duration[10]. The estimation of the mean number of divorces per marriage thus obtained shows the same shortcomings as mentioned above for the period attrition table.

We now consider *cohort analysis* of the data collected by continuous observation. The usual method is to use quotients of events in order to establish the cohort attrition table; in the case of first marriages, for example, one uses nuptiality quotients calculated each year in the generation considered, to derive from these quotients the nuptiality table in order to obtain the real intensity and tempo of first marriage, without disturbances (mortality, migration). This method unfortunately implies that each year an estimation is made of the population structure by age, sex and marital status; few countries compute these estimates each year during an inter-censal period, so that computing nuptiality quotients in longitudinal analysis is often impossible. A palliative consists in calculating reduced marriages per cohort, as defined above: the ratio of first marriages by age in a male or female cohort to the mean population (married or not) at the age considered. L. Henry has proved that if certain fundamental conditions are fulfilled[11] the sum of reduced marriages equals the average number of marriages per head, and that the weighted mean of ages (weights being the number of reduced marriages at each age) is equal to the mean age at first marriage. This approach is very interesting because it uses less elaborate data than nuptiality quotients; these measures will be frequently used in the empirical approach of paragraph III of this study. Unfortunately, this method is difficult to apply to marriage dissolutions and remarriages.

Instantaneous or retrospective observation

It is necessary to make a distinction here between censuses or surveys which ask *retrospective* questions concerning nuptiality, and *instantaneous* enumerations

9   For a general view of this problem, see N. B. Ryder, *"The process of demographic translation"*, Demography, Chicago, Vol. I, nb 1, 1964.
10 This method has been introduced by L. Henry in *"Mesure de la fréquence des divorces"*, Paris, 1952, nb 2.
11 L. Henry, *"Approximations et erreurs dans les tables de nuptialité des générations"*, Population, Paris, 1963, nb 4; G. Wunsch, *"L'utilisation des mariages réduits. Etude des perturbations introduites par la mortalité et la mobilité spatiale"*, Population et Famille, Brussels, 1970, nb 21.

giving only the status of a population at a given time. A quite precise analysis of nuptiality can be carried out when the census form includes retrospective questions on the dates of marriages and marriage-dissolutions[12]. Unfortunately, this information is rarely collected, so that usually one must solely have recourse to status statistics; in this case, distributions by age of married and unmarried individuals is particularily useful.

Under certain conditions[13], proportions of persons single at a given age, observed at the time of census, correspond to the numbers remaining single in a nuptiality table. When a series of censuses are held with short inter-censal periods, it is possible to reconstitute the nuptiality patterns of every generation over time[14]. Very frequently however, inter-censal periods are too long to apply the above method. It is then necessary to resort to period analysis, for example to the hypothetical cohort method. The percentage of persons single aged 50 (at higher ages, the number of first marriages is practically negligible) is taken as the proportion ultimately single and the proportions of persons single at each age are combined, according to J. Hajnal's method[15], to evaluate the fictitious mean age at first marriage. Like any period analysis based on the synthetic cohort method, this approach is of course influenced by the distortion effects mentioned above; it can only be used to determine the main trends of first marriage over time[16]. Let us finally mention that without retrospective questions, it is practically impossible to study marriage-dissolution and re-marriage using solely census data.

All the above mentioned methods can be applied either to females or males. They do not take into account the interaction between male and female populations[17]; to tackle this difficult problem, it would be necessary to elaborate "bisexual" marriage-rates which implies solving many methodological problems beforehand. An interesting approach to this problem has recently been developed by L. Henry[18]; waiting for a fully satisfactory solution, it is useful to complete any disjoint analysis of nuptiality of males or females with a parallel

---

12 A. Monnier and G. Stroobant op. cit.; U.S. National Center for Health Statistics: "*Needs for national studies of population dynamics*", Documents and committee reports series 4, number 12, Rockville, April 1970.
13 L. Henry, "*Approximations et erreurs dans les tables de nuptialité des génétions*", op cit.
14 J. C. Chasteland and R. Pressat, "*La Nuptialité des générations françaises depuis un siecle*", Population, Paris, 1962, nb 2.
15 J. Hajnal, "*Age at marriage and Proportions marrying*", Population Studies, London, November 1953.
16 C. Wattelar, G. Wunsch and S. Gillet-De Stefano, "*Un exemple de distorsion en analyse transversale. L'âge moyen au marriage par la méthode de Hajnal*", Recherches Economiques de Louvain, Etudes démographiques, Louvain, 1970, nb 5.
17 See in this connection P. H. Karmel, "*The relations between male and female nuptiality in a stable population*", Population Studies, London, March 1948.
18 L. Henry, "*Problèmes de nuptialité. Considérations de méthode*", Population, Paris 1968, nb 5; id., "*Schémas de nuptialité: déséquilibre des sexes et âge au mariage*", Population, Paris 1969, nb 6; id., "*Schémas de nuptialité: déséquilibre des sexes et célibat*", Population, Paris, 1969, nb 3.

study of marriageable populations presents[19]. The problem of disproportions between the sexes does not rise in the study of marriage-dissolutions, as the observation unit is, in the case, the couple rather than the individual.

B. *Data collected*

Nuptiality data collected in Europe have formed the subject of two recent studies, on which will be based what follows[20].

In the first place, it must be noted that, even if many countries collect interesting nuptiality data by means of vital statistics, the data collected leave much to be desired. In the second place, the statistics published usually make possible an appropriate study of nuptiality of persons single, based either on the proportions of persons single enumerated at the time of census, or by the method of reduced marriages. On the other hand, data on marriage-dissolutions and remarriages are much less suitable for an accurate demographic analysis. Moreover, the combined use of data dealing with population movement and status proves to be difficult outside census periods; indeed, few countries estimate the necessary inter-censal population structures for the computation of elaborate measures of analysis.

Furthermore, as mentioned above, retrospective questions necessary for nuptiality analysis based on census data have rarely been asked; sometimes, some retrospective questions have been asked, but the way the data are published makes the information unsuitable for demographic analysis. Finally, even in the industrialized countries of Europe, data collection and publication is still far from satisfactory in the field of nuptiality. More imagination of the national statistical institutes and a better knowledge of modern methods of nuptiality analysis would be highly recommended. Various tables relating to data collected and published on first marriage in European countries can be found in A. Monnier and G. Stroobant's article mentioned above.

Retaining only *published* data, we present the two following summary tables. The first table distributes various European countries according to published vital statistics and census data which make it possible to calculate the fundamental measures of analysis detailed in the above paragraph on methods of analysis: nuptiality-rates, nuptiality quotients and reduced marriages. If some countries do *collect* the necessary data, few are those which publish them in an adequate manner.

The situation is a little better concerning the sole use of census. Most European countries publish the necessary data for evaluating proportions of persons single by age and their by-products, the proportion of ultimately single and the mean age at marriage according to Hajnal's method. On the other hand, few countries publish answers to retrospective questions useful to the demo-

19 See for example D. S. Akers, *"On measuring the marriage squeeze"*, Demography, Chicago, 1967, vol. 4, nb 2.
20 B. Colombo, *"Comment améliorer les statistiques de nuptialité et de ruptures d'union"*, Recherches Economiques de Louvain, "Etudes démographiques", Louvain, 1970, nb 5; A. Monnier and G. Stroobant, op. cit.

Table I

Distribution of European countries according to published vital statistics and census data

Vital Registration	Census or estimate: Population by age (or year of birth), sex and marital status
Marriages by age, year of birth and marital status	Belgium, France, Switzerland, Denmark, Germany (F.R.)
Marriages by year of birth and marital status	Hungary, Sweden, Netherlands
Marriages by age and marital status	Spain, Finland, Luxemburg, Norway, Sweden

Source: A. Monnier and G. Stroobant, *op. cit.*, table 1.3.

grapher. Here, took the collected data are usually not published in an adequate manner.

In the field of marriage-dissolutions, data are frequently rather scanty. Most European countries publish the annual number of divorces, which enables us to use L. Henry's method of weighted averages. Fewer countries, however, publish the distribution of divorces according to duration of marriage or year of marriage; these countries are: Federal Republic of Germany, Belgium, France, Luxemburg, The Netherlands, Sweden and Great-Britain. As to widowhood according to marriage-duration or year of marriage, the following countries can be stated: Federal Republic of Germany, Switzerland, Sweden, The Netherlands, Luxemburg, Finland and France. France, Switzerland and Hungary are the only countries that annually publish the distribution of remarriages according to the duration since marriage-dissolution.

It is necessary to point out, however, that in many cases, most of these statistics are recent; it is thus very difficult, in the case of marriage-dissolutions

Table II

Distribution of European countries according to published census data

	Population by age (or year of birth), sex and marital status	Retrospective question: date of 1st marriage
Infrequent censuses	Germany (F.R.), Belgium, Luxemburg, Italy, Norway, Switzerland, Spain, Austria	Spain, England, Czechoslovakia, France
Series of sensuses or estimates	France, England, Hungary, Ireland, Sweden, Denmark, Finland, Netherlands, Czechoslovakia	

(Source: A. Monnier and G. Stroobant, *op. cit.*, table 2.3)

and remarriages, to outline the trend by cohort of the processes studied. Furthermore, population structures according to marital status and duration since marriage or marriage-dissolutions are only known at the time of census; it is thus necessary to work with synthetic period measures at the time of census or, when the necessary data have been collected for a sufficiently long time, to calculate measures obtained by dividing the number of events (marriage-dissolutions, remarriages) by the *initial* population of the cohort at the time of marriage or of marriage-dissolution.

We hope this paragraph has shown the reader the difficulty of nuptiality analysis; some problems of analysis have never been fully solved up to now and, moreover, the published data frequently remain inadequate for a rigorous analysis, mainly for the study of marriage-dissolutions and remarriages. It is thus essential to improve the quality of vital statistics in this field; one should also make a better use of retrospective questions in censuses or surveys.

III. Recent trends of first marriage

This paragraph is devoted to the analysis or recent trends of first marriage in various industrialized countries of Western Europe which have been chosen essentially for the quality of the data they publish. We shall try, as far as possible, to bring out the cohort intensity and tempo of the processes studied, among the generations married since the end of the last world war. We shall therefore only briefly outline the trend of the intensity of first marriage from the beginning of the century to the end of the second world-war; besides, these trends have already been well summarized by other authors[21]. It is sufficient to note that the general trend goes towards a decrease of average age at marriage (Hajnal's method) and of the proportions ultimately single, a trend which has however evolved rather differently for males and females. At the beginning of the century, the proportion ultimately single was clearly higher for females than for males, then the decrease of this proportion has evolved more rapidly for females, so that the difference between the proportion of males and females ultimately single has been considerably reduced over time.

It is however necessary here to take into account the variations of population structures by age and sex. Considering the age difference between spouses, one may roughly say that the decrease of mortality, and in some cases emigration[22], has led to disproportions between the sexes at the first ages at marriage, causing a notable increase of ultimately single females. Later on, the decrease of emigration and natality has considerable modified the marriage-market: the

---

21 See in particular J. Hajnal: *"The marriage boom"*, Population Index, Princeton, April 1953; J. A. Rowntree, *"Falling age at marriage and decrease of celibacy"* European Population Conference, Official Documents of the Conference, Volume I, Strasbourg, 1966; N. B. Ryder, *"Measures of recent nuptiality in the Western World"* International Union for Scientific Study of Population, New York, 1961.
22 This is the case in Norway, for example; see L. Henry, *"La population de la Norvège depuis deux siecles"*, Population, Paris 1970, nb 3.

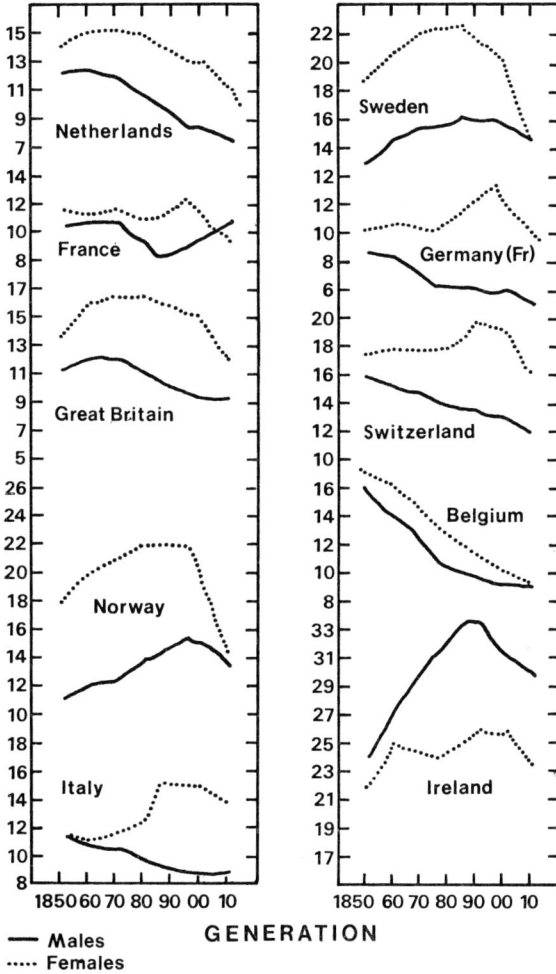

Fig.1. Proportions of ultimately single at successive censuses since 1900.

disproportion previously disfavouring the nuptiality of females tends to diminish or even to take the opposite direction, inducing a rapid decrease of the proportion of spinsters, greater than the corresponding decrease for males. The above outline naturally is very crude; differences exist in the trends between one country and another, as can be seen from figure I; in particular, France and Ireland do not follow the model outlined above[23].

Let us now examine the trends of recent cohorts which have not yet re-

23 For France, see the articles of L. Henry stated in footnote (18), published in Population, 1969, nbs 3 and 6.

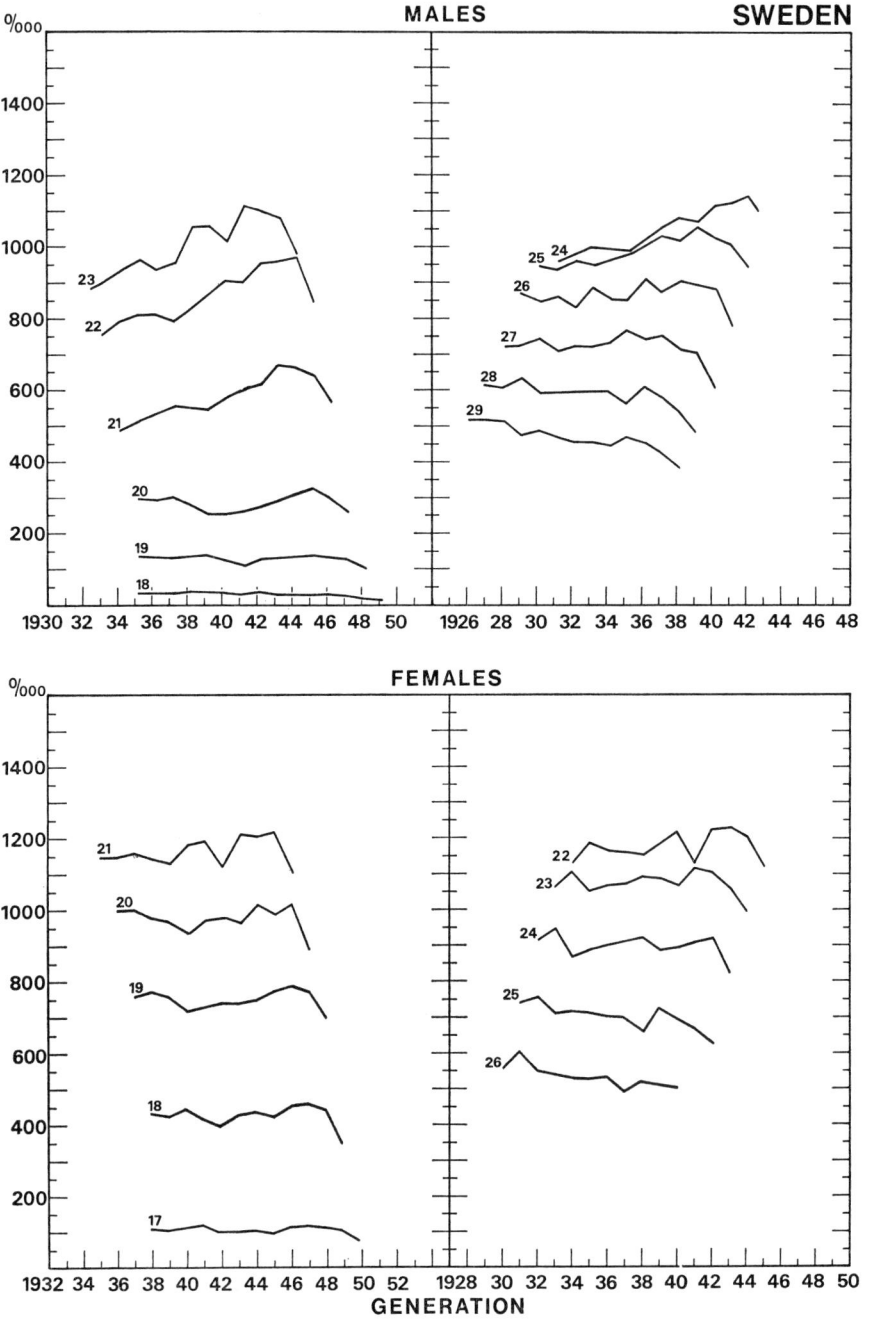

Fig. 2. Sweden. Reduced marriages by age and generation (for 10,000 males and females).

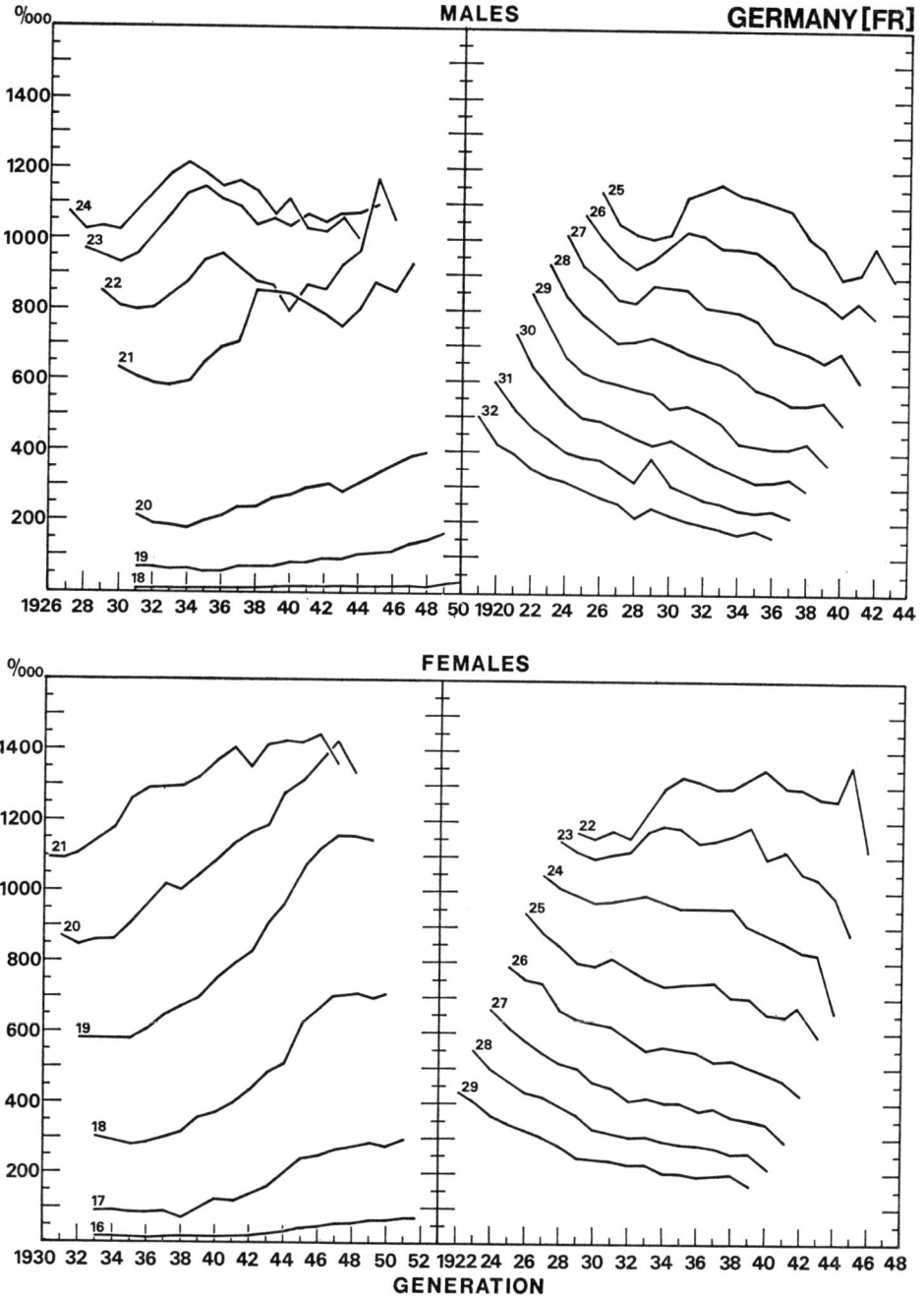

Fig. 3. Federal Republic of Germany. Reduced marriages by age and generation (for 10,000 males and females).

ached the ultimate age of marriage, roughly corresponding to 50 years of age; the method used here is that of *reduced marriages* mentioned in paragraph II above[24], making it possible to study recent cohort trends of first marriage. Six countries with adequate data have been selected: Switzerland, The Netherlands, the Federal Republic of Germany, Sweden, France and Belgium; the method used here, however, does not enable us to go back very far in time for the above countries.

Sweden

Figure 2 presents the trends of reduced marriages by age and generation for the male and female cohorts reaching marriageable age in 1955 and after.

One observes a distinct increase of male nuptiality between 21 and 25 years of age; afterwards, reduced marriages become stable or slowly decrease. For females, reduced marriages are more or less uniform at each age. At most one observes a slight increase between 20 and 22 years of age. *The modal age* of the male and female distributions remains constant, at 23–24 years of age for males, and 22 for females. These trends do not necessarily correspond to a fundamental behaviour: increase of births between 1935 and 1945 has caused an excess of women at marriageable ages, to the benefit of male nuptiality.

The decrease of the number of births between 1946 and 1960 should progressively reverse the trend and reduce male nuptiality. It is highly probable, in any case, that the disproportion between the sexes due to the increase of natality between 1935 and 1945 shall reduce the proportion of males ultimately single of the cohorts born between approximately 1932 and 1942.

Federal Republic of Germany

Figure 3, presenting male and female reduced marriages for Western Germany, immediately appears very different from the previous graph[25]. Male nuptiality decreases distinctly after 23 years of age whilst female nuptiality at young ages is in increase; this evolution, moreover, tends to reduce the *modal* age at marriage for males and females.

The complex influence of population structures by age and sex depending on the past evolution of natality and immigration is superposed upon what seems to be a fundamental change of the tempo of nuptiality towards a lowering of the mean age at marriage. The decrease of male nuptiality and the increase

---

24　We base ourselves here, completing them, on the studies undertaken at the Department of Demography of the Catholic University of Louvain v.c.l. by Mrs. Van Houte-Minet and published under the title of *"Evolution récente de la nuptialité des célibataires en pays industralisés"*, Recherches Economiques de Louvain, "Etudes démographiques", 1968, nb 4, and the book written by C. Wattelar and G. Wunsch; *"Etudes démographique, de la nuptialité en Belgique"*, Louvain, 1967 Cumulated reduced marriages by country are given as appendix.

25　The date on which are based the computation of reduced marriages do not enable us to establish perfectly homogeneous time series; see in this connection M. Van Houte-Minet, op cit. p. 457.

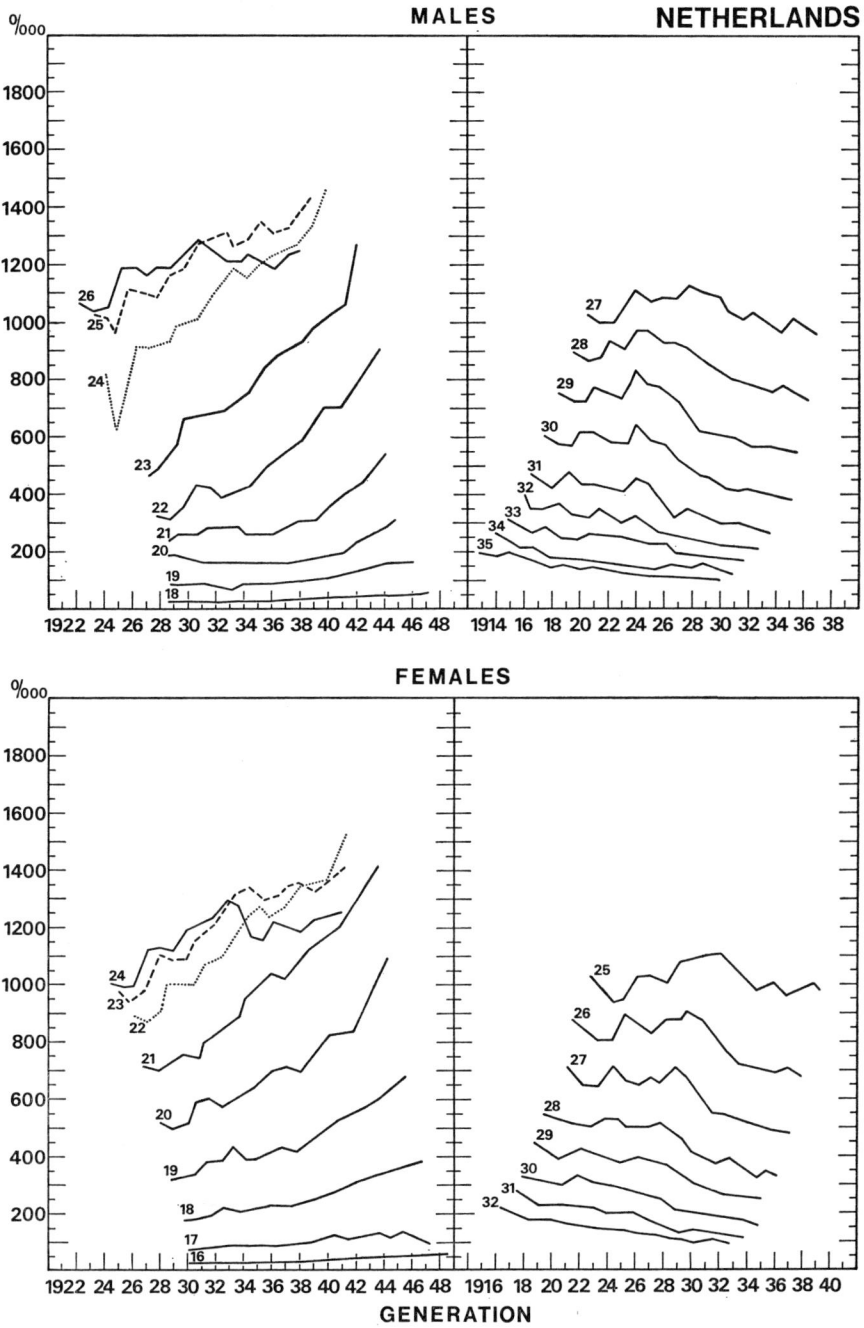

Fig. 4. The Netherlands. Reduced marriages by age and generation (for 10,000 males and females).

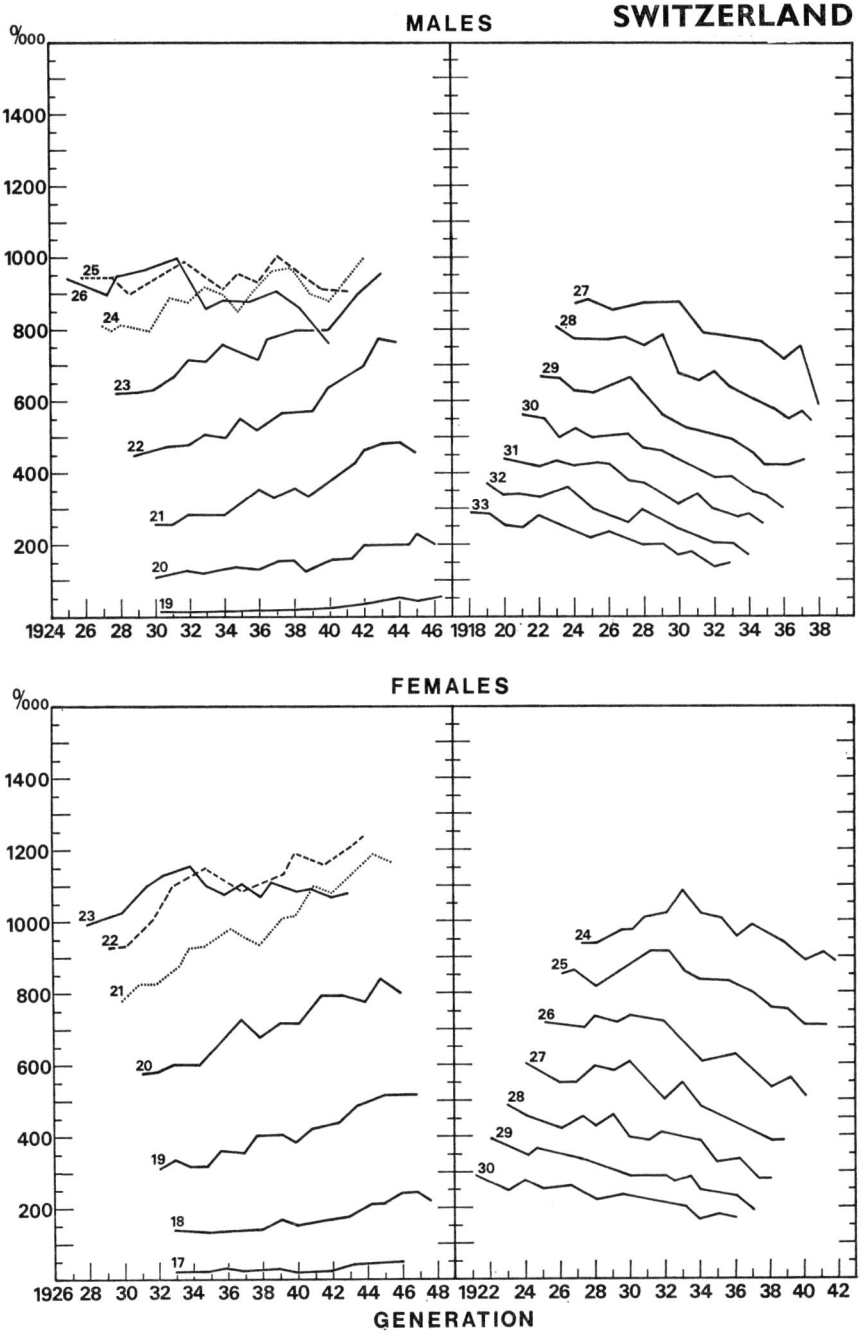

Fig. 5. Switzerland. Reduced marriages by age and generation (for 10,000 males and females).

of female nuptiality at young ages are evidently influenced by the less numerous female cohorts born during the war who reach marrigeable ages, and furthermore by arrival of young bachelors coming from East Germany.

The end of immigration and the continuous increase of births between 1953 and 1963 will eventually moderate the female advantage on the marriage-market. It seems probable that female cohorts at present at marriageable ages will experience an increase of the final intensity of nuptiality; if one adds up *reduced events* in order to obtain *incomplete intensities* of nuptiality before 50 years of age, one notices (see appendix) a constant increase of these sums from one generation to another at every age. It is, however, impossible to draw a similar conclusion for male cohorts, except for the generations born during the pre-war economic depression.

The Netherlands

As shown in figure 4, the variations in intensity and tempo are particularily notable in the Netherlands: sharp decline in age at marriage and, cumulating reduced marriages (see appendix), increase of incomplete intensities, this being a probable indication of a decrease in the proportions ultimately single in the female and male generations.

This trend reduces from 24 to 22 years of age the female *modal* age at marriage (generations 1933 to 1940); the male *modal age* has also decreased by one year if one compares the distributions relating to birth-cohorts 1930 and 1938. This clearly shows a radical change of attitude of the young generations towards marriage, independently of possible disproportions of sexes on the marriage-market[26].

Switzerland

The variations of nuptiality of young generations in Switzerland are very similar to those of the Netherlands, though less accentuated.

Here too, the male and female *modal* age at marriage decreases. Contrary to the Netherlands, however, the change in tempo of nuptiality does not accompany a marked increase in the intensity of marriage, as one can observe by cumulating reduced marriages (see appendix).

France

We shall only briefly outline the French situation, as various other studies have already dealt with this problem[27]. Briefly, cohort analysis shows an in-

---

26 This "market" has generally been unfavourable to female marriage; even so, female nuptiality is clearly increasing, as one can see in the appendix.

27 A. Nizard and R. Pressat, *"La situation démographique"*, Population, Paris, 1965, nb 4; G. Calot and S. Hemery, *"L'évolution de la situation démographique française au cours des années récentes"*; Population, Paris, 1967, nb 4; id.: *"La fécondité et la nuptialité en 1966 et 1967"*, Population, Paris, nb 6; G. Calot, S. Hémery and C. Piro, *"L'évolution récente de la fécondité et de la nuptialité en France"*, Population, Paris 1969, nb 2: R. Pressat, *"La conjoncture démographique"*, Population, Paris, 1970, nb 2.

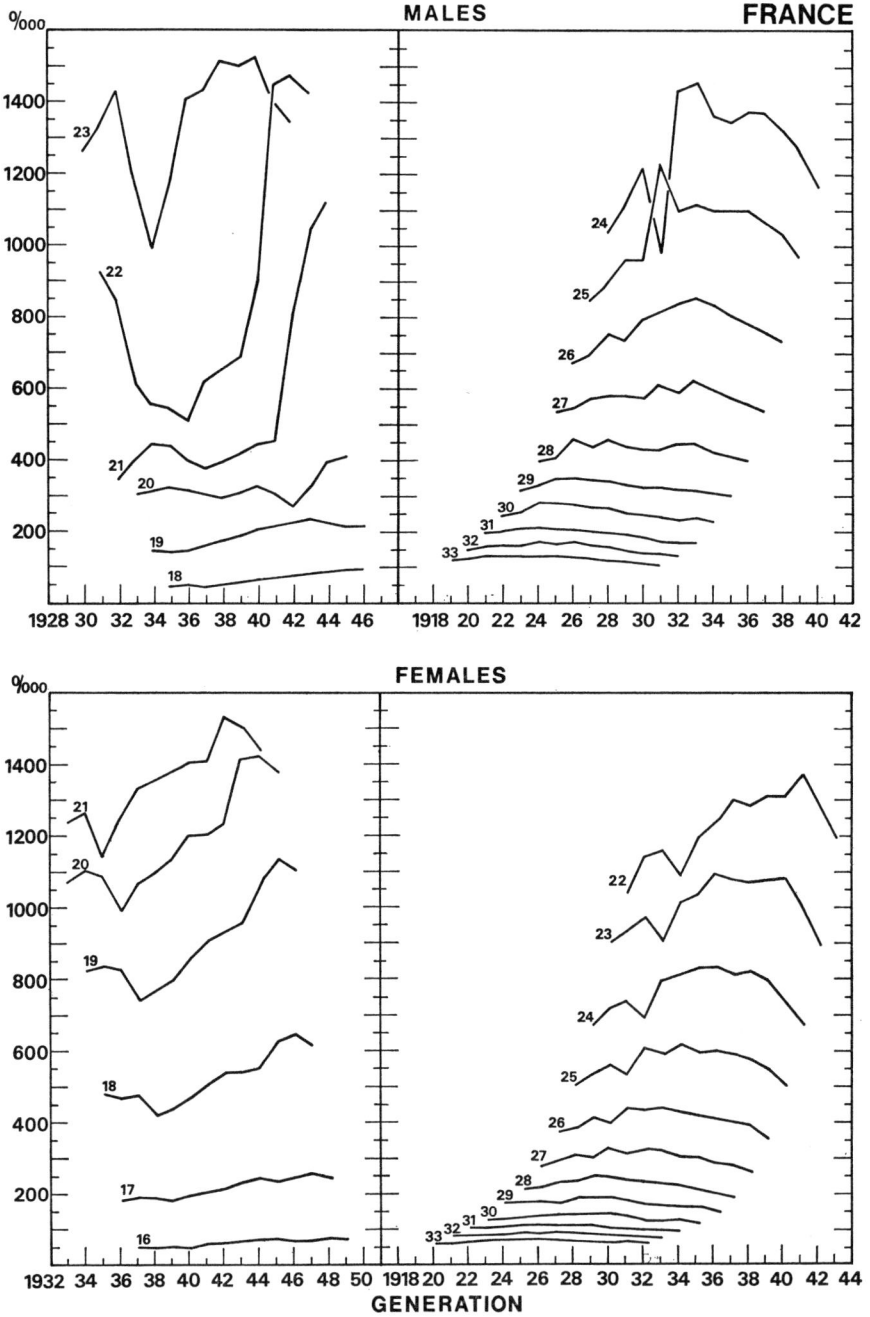

Fig. 6. France. Reduced marriages by age and generation (for 10,000 males and females).

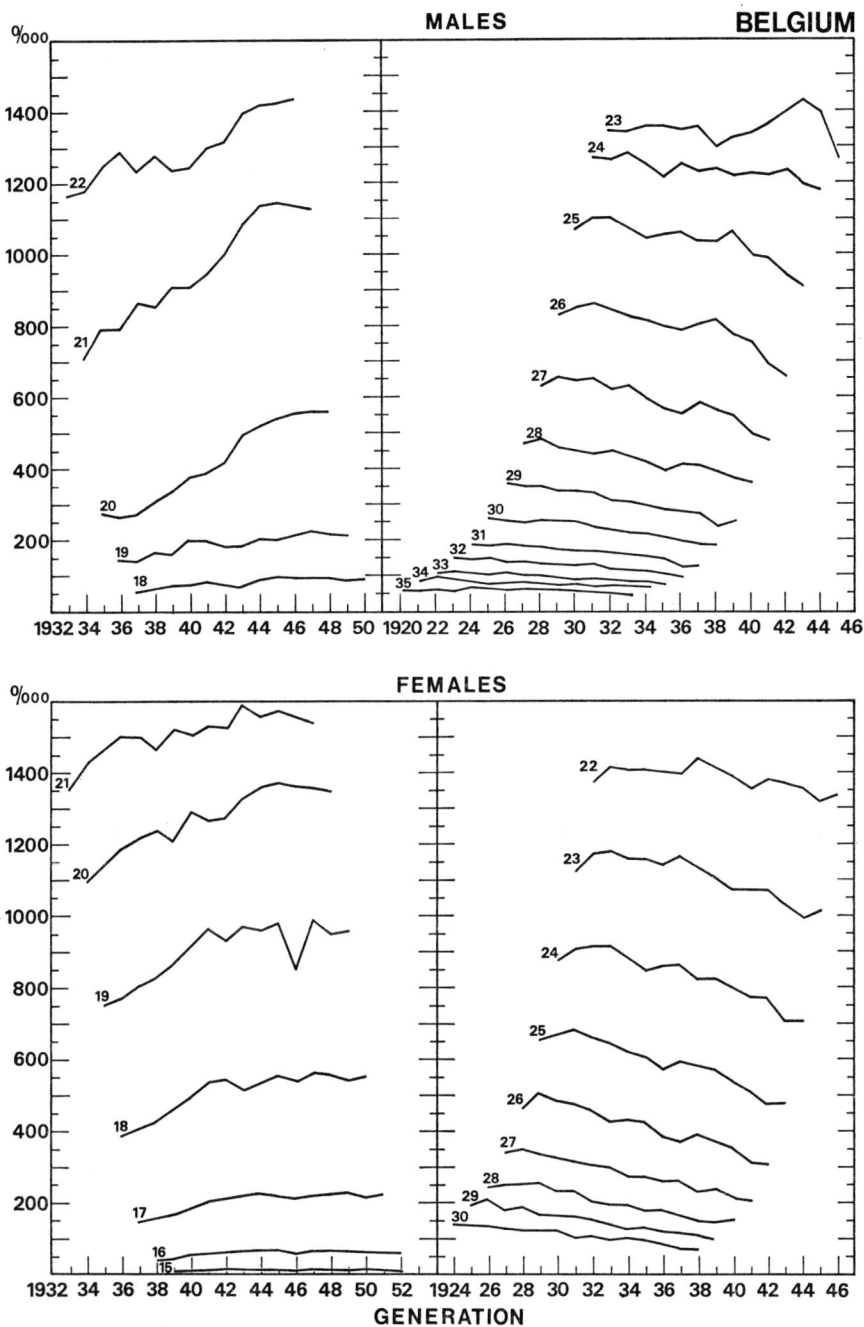

Fig. 7. Belgium. Reduced marriages by age and generation (for 10,000 males and females).

crease in marriage at younger ages in male generations born between 1937 and 1942 and even more clearly in female birth-cohorts born between 1940–1945 (see appendix).

Up to 1964, nuptiality increased regularly for males and females; since then, nuptiality indices have rapidly decreased. It seems that this trend depends on a delay in age at marriage amongst recent generations or, what seems more probable, on the end of the decrease of age at marriage. Let us also note the influence of the marriage-market: females of the numerous generations born after 1945, usually marry males of the less numerous generations born before 1946; they will thus temporarily experience a reduced intensity of marriage.

Belgium

Here too, analysis shows a trend to younger age at marriage, reduced marriages for males and females increasing at young ages and decreasing at higher ages.

This change in tempo of nuptiality is once more very probably accompanied by an increase in the intensity of nuptiality of recent generations, as seen in the appendix presenting a cumulated form of male and female cohort reduced marriages.

On the whole, cohort analysis has shown an almost general trend towards younger age at first marriage, very often indicating the real propensity of younger generations towards marriage, rather than a transitory effect due to disproportions on the marriage-market for example. Besides, the decrease in age at marriage is often accompanied by a greater intensity of marriage by cohort; this is clearly the case in the Netherlands[28].

It is evident that such a trend cannot go on much longer; the decrease in period measures at present observed in certain countries indicates the end of the trend towards a lower age at marriage and a higher intensity of first marriage.

IV. Recent trends of marriage-dissolution and remarriage

Ideally, the study of recent trends of marriage-dissolution should be based on cohort attrition tables of marriage by widowhood or divorce, by duration of marriage and age of the spouses, with a view to evaluate the probability of marriage-dissolution at each duration of marriage. The statistics published, however, rarely enable one to have recourse to such an analysis. Nevertheless, different palliatives can be used to show the present impact of marriage-dissolution on nuptiality in Europe.

Firstly, with relation to widowhood, one can say that its impact is at present rather small in the industrialized countries of Europe, at least at fertile ages, the only ages interesting us here. Marriages dissolved by widowhood at

---

28 For this country, see B. W. Frijling, H. J. Heeren, H. G. Moors and R. van der Vlist, "*De dalende huwelijksleeftijd. Sociologische en demografische beschouwingen*", Sociologische Gids, Sept.-Oct. 1969, reprint nb 59 of the Sociologisch Instituut, Rijksuniversiteit, Utrecht.

fertile ages are most often due to the husband's death; this results from the age
difference at time of marriage between spouses (the husband usually being
older than his wife) as well as from the excess mortality of men as compared
with women of the same age. Secondly, as the timing of births nowadays occurs
in a relatively short duration of marriage and, on an average, at relatively
young ages, the impact of widowhood on natality is rather limited at the present time. By means of a model based on period Swiss data, A. Meli and E.
Huelsen have demonstrated[29], in the connection, that marriages dissolved by
the deaths of the husband or of the wife would anyhow give *birth to 77% of the
fertility* which would have been observed in the absence of widowhood; on the

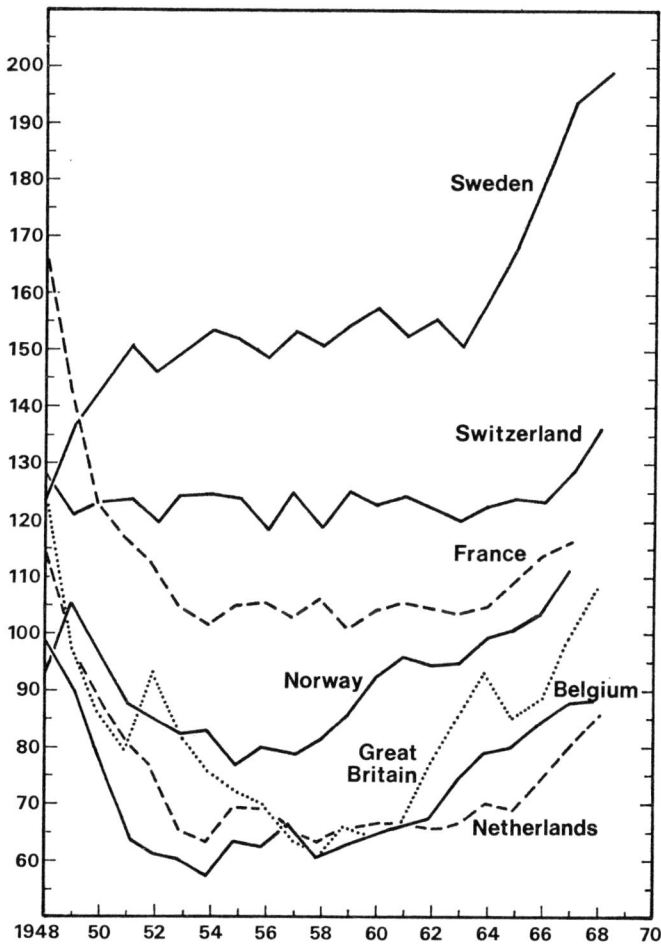

Fig. 8. Mean number of divorces per thousand marriages (weighted mean method).

29 A. Meli and E. Huelsen, "*Sur les ruptures d'union*", European Population Conference, Vol.
    I, Strasbourg, 1966.

contrary, marriages dissolved by divorce only give birth *to 48% of the fertility* that would have been observed without divorce. Divorce, contrary to widowhood, affects marriage of rather short durations. Basing his research on period German statistics, K. Schwarz has demonstrated[30], for example, that 60% of the marriages that only last 10 years are dissolved by divorce.

Considering the present-day extent of divorce, it is useful to characterize its evolution amongst recent cohorts. We will use L. Henry's method of weighted means, adapted to take into account the differential distribution of divorces by duration of marriage between the different countries[31]. The results of this computation are presented in figure VIII for seven industrialized countries of Western Europe.

Briefly mentioning the increase of divorce-rates just after the second world-war, the period divorce indices appear clearly to increase in the last few years. A longitudinal analysis of divorce according to duration of marriage, which should complete the previous analysis, is made difficult by the fact that, most of the time, the necessary data (divorces classified annually according to duration of marriage) are not available over a long period of time. A few partial data relating to Great Britain and Sweden[32], Austria[33] and Czechoslovakia[34] seem to confirm the trend towards a greater intensity of the mean number of divorces per marriage. It may be possible that, in some cases, it might only be the effect of a modification of the divorce tempo, tending towards a lowering of age at divorce; in any case, the Swedish data on marriage cohorts from 1941 to 1950 indicate both an increase of intensity of divorce as well as a trend towards younger age at divorce.

On the whole, one sees that over the last 20 years, the decrease of probabilities of widowhood has been compensated by an increase of probabilities of divorce; this follows the trend observed for many years in certain European countries[35].

Finally, here is a brief view of the recent trends of remarriage[36]; here too, the lack of data makes analysis difficult and one is forced, in practice, to use only period analysis, except in the case of France, which has good statistics on

---

30   K. Schwarz, *"L'histoire d'une génération avec ses enfants et petits-enfants"*, Recherches Economiques de Louvain, "Etudes démographiques", 1969, nb 4.
31   See in this connection M. Van Houte-Minet, *"Analyse longitudinale de la nuptialité des célibataires et du divorce"*, International Union for the Scientific Study of Population, General Conference, London, September 1969.
32   M. Van Houten-Minet, op. cit.
33   H. Hansluwka, "Divorces in Austria", International Symposium on the problems of human reproduction, Varna, Bulgaria, Sept. 1968.
34   M. Kučera, *"Divorce rate according to the duration of marriage"*, Demosta, Praque, 2–1968-II.
35   In Belgium, for example, the increase of divortiality continues since the beginning of the century, the average number of divorces per marriage (by the weighted-average method) increasing progressively from 16‰ in 1900 to 82‰ in 1965. See: C. Wattelar and G. Wunsch, *"Etude démographique de la nuptialité en Belgique"*, op. cit. p. 56–61.
36   Data are taken from the study by M. Van Houte-Minet, *"La remariage en pays industrialisés. Approches transversale et longitudinale"*, Recherches Economiques de Louvain, "Etudes démographiques", Louvain, 1969, no 4.

Table III

Standardized age-specific indices (%) of the remarriage of
widows and divorcées for various calander years

Country	Widows					
England and Wales (1)	1956 13.3	1958 12.0	1960 13.5	1962 11.5	1964 11.0	1966 10.3
France (2)	1954/55 7.8	1957/58 8.2	1960/61 8.4	1962/63 8.1	1964/65 7.8	
Netherlands (2)	1954/55 10.3	1958/59 11.15	1960/61 8.0	1962/63 7.5	1964/65 8.6	
Sweden (2)	1955/56 11.9	1958/59 6.9	1961/62 6.2	1963/64 5.8	1965/66 4.9	
Switzerland (2)	1950/51 10.2		1960/61 6.9			
Federal Republic of Germany (2)	1950/51 12.7		1961 6.6			
Belgium (3)	1955 11.1	1958 9.6	1960 8.9	1963 8.0	1965 7.9	

Country	Divorcées					
England and Wales (1)	1956 21.7	1958 20.2	1960 21.3	1962 21.8	1964 22.3	1966 21.9
France (2)	1954/55 13.5	1957/58 13.7	1960/61 14.4	1962/63 14.2	1964/65 14.6	
Netherlands (2)	1954/55 18.3	1958/59 18.5	1960/61 18.7	1962/63 18.6	1964/65 18.0	
Sweden (2)	1955/56 17.9	1958/59 17.0	1961/62 16.6	1963/64 15.4	1965/66 14.1	
Switzerland (2)	1950/51 13.8		1960/61 13.0			
Federal Republic of Germany (2)	1950/51 18.5		1961 15.6			
Belgium (3)	1955 11.2	1958 11.8	1960 11.7	1963 12.0	1965 13.4	

(1) Females aged 25 to 44 years.
(2) Females aged 20 to 44 years.
(3) Females aged 20 to 64 years.

remarriage. Standardized indices of remarriage by age[37] show a decrease of remarriage of widows during the last ten to twenty years in a few European countries (except in France, where the indices remain stable) and stability in female divorcées remarriage, except in France where indices slightly increase and in Sweden where they decrease. In the latter country, this trend parallels the low female intensity of first marriage mentioned above; whereas to France,

---

37 These indices were computed for the female population at fertile ages, remarriages at more advanced ages not being of interest to the demographer in so far as they do not affect natality. Detailed tables are given in the article by M. Van Houte-Minet op cit.

the detailed analysis made by M. Van Houte-Minet shows that this is probably only a temporary behaviour resulting from a lack of females single on the
marriage-market.

The above table is of course very crude; it takes into account only age, and
not the demographic structure by marital status, so that its interpretation remains difficult. It seems, however, that on the whole during the last twenty
years one can observe in various industrialized European countries a decrease
of nuptiality of widows and a stability in remarriage of divorcées, amongst the
women of reproductive ages: of course, where as to widows, the decrease may
be partly fictitious: in so far as mortality decreases, widowhood tends more and
more to occur at ages where the probability of marriage is low. As to the remarriage of divorcées, as we have noticed in France, one should take into account the disproportion between sexes on the marriage market, because the
number of remarriages is evidently influenced by the conditions of first marriage. Without more elaborate data on this matter, it is difficult to have an
exact idea of the real trends of remarriage in the industrialized countries of
Europe.

V. Summary and conclusions

After noting that nuptiality interests the demographer essentially for its
impact on natality and thus on population movements, we have briefly summarized the methods of analysis used in the field of nuptiality, and this for
various reasons. Firstly, data collection should be a function of methods used;
secondly, certain recent techniques (such as reduced marriages) are still badly
known, especially by American demographers; finally, each method has its
limits which should be kept in mind when proceeding to empirical analysis of
the data.

The analysis of data collected in Europe has shown us that nuptiality still
often remains a neglected field. This is mostly the case in the study of marriage-
dissolutions and, even more, of remarriages. The lack of adequate data pre-
venting the best use of the resources of demographic analysis, the empirical
analysis of nuptiality will necessarily stay incomplete and schematic.

In the case of first marriages, firstly, the analysis for a few industrialized
European countries shows – on the whole – the continuation of the previous
trends, reduction of celibacy and increasing precocity of marriage. However,
during the last 20 years, this trend hardly depends, as it did previously, on the
composition of the eligible population; on the contrary, it seems to correspond
to the fundamental behaviour of young generations towards nuptiality. This
movement towards a greater precocity and intensity cannot, however, go on
very long, except in some country or other such as Switzerland, where nuptiality is still relatively late, so that one must expect a stabilization of the trend for
recent generations; the decrease of period measures observed recently in certain countries tends to confirm this hypothesis. In the field of marriage-dissolutions, a few partial results confirm the hypothesis of the rather small impact

of widowhood at fertile ages at the present time. As to divorce, it seems to increase in most of the countries studied, even if one takes into account, on the other hand, the greater precocity of divorces which also seems to take place. Let us note, furthermore, that the study of Mrs. Van Houte-Minet establishes an age-effect on marriage stability: it seems that divorces are all the more frequent as the women of a same marriage cohort were married younger. However, the lack of adequate data has not made it possible to extend this analysis to various European countries.

The results concerning remarriages are unfortunately extremely sketchy. In most cases, one can just eliminate only the influence of age structure in period analysis; in this case, one observes a decrease in the nuptiality of widows and stability in that of divorcées. A closer study based on the sole French data shows a rather great stability, in intensity as well as in tempo, of remarriage among widows, young widows remarrying sooner than older ones, as well as an increase of nuptiality among divorcées which however, can be due simply to population structures. We must, of course, take care not to extrapolate these results to other countries.

To bring this article to a conclusion, one may say that most industrialized countries of Europe have attained or will attain a very low level of celibacy and a young age at marriage, as also observed in the U.S.A. for example, a process which is also on a par with a greater intensity of divorce. The position of Western Europe is thus fundamentally different for the moment, from what it was in the 19th and at the beginning of the 20th century. To estimate the impact of this trend on the demographic situation in Europe, one must only think of what would be the crude birth-rate and rate of increase, already so low at present in European countries, if their populations should offer the same nuptiality characteristics as their ancestors. May be, therefore one should luckily reverse the statement by Malthus[38] and write "however powerful may be the impulses of reason, they are generally in some degree modified by passion".

Acknowledgments

I wish to thank my colleagues at the Department of Demography of the University of Louvain (U.C.L.), especially Mrs. G. Stroobant-Masuy and Miss C. Wattelar, for reading the manuscript and making several suggestions.

I also wish to acknowledge the financial support given by the Belgian national fund for scientific research and by the I.U.S.S.P., which has enabled my Department to carry out various studies on marriage and marriage dissolution in industrialized countries during the last few years.

---

38 *On population*, The Modern Library, Random House, New York, 1960, p. 497.

Appendix I. SWEDEN: Cumulated reduced marriages by age and generation.

(for 10.000 males)

Age	\multicolumn{15}{c}{Year of birth}

Age	1935	1936	1937	1938	1939	1940	1941	1942	1943	1944	1945	1946	1947	1948	1949
18	29*	30*	30	32	30	31	25	31	24	25	26	29	30	18	15
19	157*	156	153	163	166	152	131	155	154	157	164	159	151	110	
20	448	443	445	437	416	402	388	425	443	467	488	459	408		
21	958	973	995	983	957	977	982	1037	1112	1128	1129	1023			
22	1761	1781	1779	1803	1818	1879	1879	1989	2065	2096	1969				
23	2716	2709	2722	2851	2867	2885	2989	3082	3142	3069					
24	3701	3727	3776	3932	3937	4007	4116	4227	4170						
25	4682	4738	4812	4352	5000	5044	5122	5173							
26	5536	5643	5683	5853	5894	5924	5894								
27	6306	6340	6436	6569	6603	6538									
28	6869	6953	7018	7112	7085										
29	7339	7407	7444	7494											

(for 10.000 females)

Age	\multicolumn{14}{c}{Year of birth}

Age	1938	1939	1940	1941	1942	1943	1944	1945	1946	1947	1948	1949	1950	1951
16	12*	12*	11	13	13	9	7	9	9	10	8	11	11	8
17	111*	109	113	123	105	100	102	100	113	118	112	107	81	
18	532	522	546	528	490	517	526	513	556	567	546	452		
19	1293	1270	1251	1246	1220	1245	1264	1284	1335	1328	1237			
20	2256	2223	2172	2206	2183	2200	2271	2252	2342	2208				
21	3386	3340	3344	3387	3288	3402	3469	3459	3429					
22	4535	4522	4559	4516	4510	4626	4672	4570						
23	5621	5602	5614	5616	5609	5684	5670							
24	6534	6481	6502	6520	6523	6504								
25	7187	7204	7195	7184	7153									
26	7703	7712	7688	7646										

*Estimate.

Appendix II. GERMANY (FR) Cumulated reduced marriages by age and generation.

(for 10.000 males)

Year of birth

Age	1931	1932	1933	1934	1935	1936	1937	1938	1939	1940	1941	1942	1943	1944	1945	1946	1947	1948	1949	1950
18	8*	9*	9	8	10	7	8	8	10	11	13	13	14	15	17	16	18	20	28	32
19	73*	74	70	74	68	69	83	82	85	99	103	109	110	117	129	133	154	167	199	
20	290	270	254	259	268	290	329	331	351	387	397	413	398	426	465	496	539	544		
21	896	857	841	856	919	984	1046	1182	1243	1236	1223	1205	1148	1232	1343	1346	1466			
22	1695	1663	1676	1734	1862	1939	1965	2086	2110	2033	2095	2062	2075	2201	2511	2400				
23	2656	2669	2742	2859	3007	3047	3105	3126	3171	3069	3162	3109	3140	3272	3606					
24	3732	3803	3926	4075	4191	4251	4271	4268	4236	4179	4191	4130	4204	4218						
25	4860	4947	5081	5208	5366	5356	5360	5285	5223	5080	5005	5124	5095							
26	5890	5960	6062	6235	6338	6296	6240	6140	6059	5876	5828	5908								
27	6755	6777	6906	7042	7120	7017	6946	6829	6723	6556	6432									
28	7435	7463	7560	7670	7697	7578	7489	7368	7272	7040										
29	7994	7979	8046	8109	8126	7990	7902	7791	7649											
30	8401	8358	8402	8443	8442	8307	8227	8080												
31	8692	8626	8657	8682	8677	8547	8446													
32	8897	8820	8842	8857	8855	8707														

(for 10.000 females)

Year of birth

Age	1933	1934	1935	1936	1937	1938	1939	1940	1941	1942	1943	1944	1945	1946	1947	1948	1949	1950	1951	1952
16	13*	14*	14	12	13	14	15	20	20	22	29	38	45	47	56	56	61	60	65	64
17	103*	105	102	96	101	85	114	140	139	160	195	232	277	291	321	330	341	337	361	
18	405	393	383	384	401	406	466	508	539	616	679	744	894	950	1025	1038	1039	1045		
19	986	974	964	986	1050	1080	1160	1256	1362	1443	1580	1710	1955	2068	2177	2195	2186			
20	1846	1836	1875	1944	2063	2081	2204	2385	2495	2609	2761	2985	3266	3430	3605	3535				
21	2980	3013	3134	3231	3355	3376	3579	3754	3900	3960	4172	4407	4686	4871	4971					
22	4203	4307	4460	4549	4654	4728	4906	5099	5202	5261	5443	5672	6045	5990						
23	5366	5494	5640	5693	5849	5692	6086	6208	6321	6314	6484	6664	6931							
24	6356	6468	6594	6687	6806	6847	6996	7093	7185	7152	7309	7322								
25	7116	7206	7364	7429	7549	7556	7700	7752	7838	7818	7851									
26	7671	7793	7925	7981	8074	8081	8209	8235	8310	8247										
27	8105	8199	8326	8361	8461	8447	8570	8580	8609											
28	8409	8492	8607	8643	8735	8709	8830	8800												
29	8635	8701	8814	8843	8937	8910	9000													
30					9088	9043														

*Estimate

GUILLAUME WUNSCH

Appendix III. NETHERLANDS: Cumulated reduced marriages by age and generation.

(for 10.000 males)

Year of birth

Age	1927	1928	1929	1930	1931	1932	1933	1934	1935	1936	1937	1938	1939	1940	1941	1942	1943	1944	1945	1946	1947
18	18*	17*	18*	18	20	20	18	16	20	18	21	24	24	29	31	38	42	45	49	50	51
19	89*	87*	89	91	88	84	89	81	92	94	98	108	118	134	153	171	191	197	215	216	
20	272*	268	254	248	254	240	256	250	259	251	268	289	301	328	388	421	456	480	544		
21	513	532	512	534	531	513	515	510	525	538	574	595	634	709	799	869	954	1017			
22	834	900	956	965	931	949	967	1012	1052	1094	1151	1226	1333	1410	1581	1731	1891				
23	1389	1562	1628	1635	1611	1676	1739	1869	1932	1990	2085	2223	2367	2476	2776	3012					
24	2301	2472	2551	2606	2604	2744	2352	3032	3080	3166	3318	3482	3640	3828	4232						
25	3364	3531	3688	3758	3860	4014	4148	4277	4351	4496	4489	4793	4999	5238							
26	4486	4692	4839	4971	5139	5250	5328	5447	5566	5678	5477	6005	6222								
27	5570	5765	5968	6073	6227	6270	6314	6456	6539	6619	6203	6953									
28	6502	6700	6862	6916	7039	7057	7099	7465	7267	7368											
29	7271	7425	7531	7519	7634	7643	7669	8008	7815	7897											
30	7844	7938	8005	7969	8083	8058	8073	8423	8199												
31	8216	8270	8346	8294	8390	8359	8370	8702													
32	8466	8514	8579	8519	8601	8575	8581														
33	8648	8690	8751	8682	8762	8729															

(for 10.000 females)

Year of birth

Age	1930	1931	1932	1933	1934	1935	1936	1937	1938	1939	1940	1941	1942	1943	1944	1945	1946	1947	1948	1949	1950
15	–*	–*	1*	–	1	–	1	1	1	–	1	–	1	1	1	2	2	2	2	3	2
16	12*	13*	14	14	17	17	19	21	18	21	20	26	30	31	33	40	41	39	40	43	
17	72*	75	85	92	96	93	100	100	104	111	112	139	152	147	155	179	171	187	183		
18	253	256	277	308	304	297	316	325	324	346	365	403	427	451	471	511	515	560			
19	584	594	662	694	740	696	718	741	769	782	837	925	970	1006	1053	1140	1165				
20	1089	1171	1251	1257	1330	1320	1372	1441	1484	1491	1614	2089	1825	1872	2007	2182					
21	1898	1964	2064	2105	2230	2295	2381	2505	2530	2575	2761	3478	3019	3172	3383						
22	2890	2950	3123	3187	3400	3542	3661	3752	3802	3925	4114	4867	4498	4730							
23	3988	4131	4326	4453	4741	4897	4966	5069	5163	5299	5457	6256	5938								
24	5172	5331	5565	5748	6002	6078	6131	6290	6369	6487	6684	7490									
25	6249	6430	6660	6805	7003	7046	7122	7224	7323	7469	7626										
26	7167	7314	7474	7566	7731	7759	7814	7901	8021	8134											
27	7834	7920	8013	8097	8239	8249	8294	8377	8485												
28	8271	8316	8389	8470	8590	8581	8635	8702													
29	8563	8598	8655	8715	8830	8811	8863														
30	8770	8794	8836	8893	9007	8965															

*Estimate.

Appendix IV. SWITZERLAND : Cumulated reduced marriages by age and generation.

(for 10.000 males)

Age	1930	1931	1932	1933	1934	1935	1936	1937	1938	1939	1940	1941	1942	1943	1944	1945	1946	1947	1948
18	3	2	3	3	5	5	6	6	6	9	9	6	6	9	11	12	12	12	9
19	33	33	35	37	40	42	42	39	47	44	48	48	57	65	74	70	70	73	
20	159	161	172	167	170	191	189	203	209	182	205	226	268	279	292	303	291		
21	429	430	464	463	464	513	542	542	567	520	578	643	733	767	779	772			
22	892	910	947	977	973	1072	1076	1105	1145	1104	1214	1301	1425	1541	1540				
23	1533	1580	1673	1687	1725	1806	1803	1885	1945	1904	2012	2151	2322	2501					
24	2342	2472	2553	2611	2626	2657	2689	2849	2922	2806	2892	3097	3332						
25	3280	3442	3530	3559	3536	3603	3603	3840	3896	3720	3798	4013							
26	4261	4435	4448	4410	4415	4474	4495	4753	4772	4524	4548								
27	5127	5227	5231	5184	5191	5237	5213	5496	5477	5142									
28	5810	5881	5899	5822	5814	5812	5773	6071	6036										
29	6354	6405	6410	6326	6292	6245	6207	6516											
30	6795	6822	6800	6722	6649	6586	6511												
31	7113	7161	7098	7002	6935	6840													
32	7364	7398	7315	7218	7128														
33	7546	7583	7471	7382															

(for 10.000 females)

Age	1933	1934	1935	1936	1937	1938	1939	1940	1941	1942	1943	1944	1945	1946	1947	1948
16	–	1	1	–	–	1	1	–	1	1	–	1	2	2	5	7
17	24	24	28	29	21	30	24	28	36	33	30	37	52	50	58	59
18	174	169	164	172	171	180	196	189	209	211	220	257	274	298	305	284
19	507	489	484	527	520	573	586	567	630	646	702	747	790	809	822	
20	1118	1096	1110	1201	1249	1246	1300	1280	1393	1437	1591	1624	1729	1713		
21	1984	2028	2054	2177	2193	2186	2304	2302	2482	2514	2716	2813	2894			
22	3071	3147	3196	3291	3266	3278	3426	3490	3628	3671	3927	4055				
23	4212	4299	4294	4361	4374	4346	4550	4563	4714	4742	5008					
24	5292	5309	5302	5315	5358	5303	5491	5455	5632	5643						
25	6155	6148	6137	6141	6162	6060	6236	6166	6348							
26	6832	6764	6762	6782	6744	6604	6798	6680								
27	7369	7249	7235	7233	7167	6997	7192									
28	7768	7626	7570	7568	7462	7285										
29	8054	7882	7813	7807	7665											
30	8267	8064	8001	7977												

Appendix V. FRANCE: Cumulated reduced marriages by age and generation.

(for 10.000 males)

Age	Year of birth												
	1935	1936	1937	1938	1939	1940	1941	1942	1943	1944	1945	1946	1947
18	46	47	46	49	55	64	69	74	80	88	92	94	87
19	189	196	208	223	238	286	282	301	311	311	306	310	
20	514	516	509	518	547	609	586	570	632	707	712		
21	953	909	886	914	968	1051	1035	1356	1666	1827			
22	1495	1415	1503	1564	1648	1941	2477	2820	3080				
23	2669	2810	2926	3074	3146	3460	3875	4157					
24	4022	4146	4295	4437	4466	4718	5028						
25	5114	5239	5385	5493	5489	5675							
26	5943	6044	6160	6249	6224								
27	6540	6617	6711	6779									
28	6956	7025	7108										
29	7260	7318											
30	7485												

(for 10.000 females)

Age	Year of birth												
	1937	1938	1939	1940	1941	1942	1943	1944	1945	1946	1947	1948	1949
16	56	55	59	57	66	67	70	77	77	70	73	77	75
17	249	245	239	254	272	287	305	319	312	316	327	323	
18	722	669	680	726	776	828	852	974	936	960	946		
19	1467	1441	1477	1595	1684	1760	1809	2046	2070	2067			
20	2531	2529	2618	2796	2887	3001	3228	3470	3457				
21	3862	3881	3996	4204	4296	4544	4738	4901					
22	5167	5167	5310	5517	5667	5829	5933						
23	6244	6241	6388	6598	6637	6725							
24	7062	7063	7185	7331	7339								
25	7645	7637	7733	7835									
26	8051	8034	8092										
27	8335	8304											
28	8527												

Appendix VI. BELGIUM: Cumulated reduced marriages by age and generation.

(for 10.000 males)

Age						Year of birth								
	1938	1939	1940	1941	1942	1943	1944	1945	1946	1947	1948	1949	1950	1951
17	6	7	8	9	8	8	10	9	8	9	12	12	9	10
18	69	82	83	90	85	81	101	104	102	103	109	97	97	
19	233	242	276	284	267	269	303	304	316	330	321	309		
20	545	576	652	669	683	759	816	844	869	888	878			
21	1397	1479	1556	1611	1679	1839	1949	1985	2001	2012				
22	2676	2714	2794	2902	2989	3228	3362	3401	3432					
23	3974	4037	4132	4260	4381	4654	4754	4662						
24	5215	5257	5316	5481	5617	5853	5933							
25	6248	6319	6355	6470	6560	6763								
26	7061	7091	7110	7168	7221									
27	7619	7636	7599	7640										
28	8000	8003	7954											
29	8247	8256												
30	8429													
31														

(for 10.000 females)

Age						Year of birth									
	1939	1940	1941	1942	1943	1944	1945	1946	1947	1948	1949	1950	1951	1952	1953
15	9	9	9	11	11	11	12	10	12	12	11	13	12	10	10
16	48	61	69	71	76	78	73	65	78	79	73	75	72	68	
17	213	246	276	283	295	304	287	274	299	303	302	290	296		
18	671	744	814	823	812	840	842	813	861	861	844	843			
19	1538	1662	1779	1754	1785	1799	1821	1664	1852	1810	1803				
20	2746	2950	3047	3026	3112	3160	3192	3025	3209	3158					
21	4266	4452	4576	4554	4696	4713	4768	4583	4749						
22	5683	5845	5937	5935	6068	6070	6091	5923							
23	6793	6923	7015	7012	7107	7079	7111								
24	7622	7727	7792	7788	7822	7795									
25	8198	8266	8307	8269	8303										
26	8571	8625	8626	8587											
27	8813	8846	8836												
28	8965	9004													
29	9071														

Some Notes on the Changing Fertility in Europe and the Study of it

BERNHARD FRIJLING

Utrecht

I

THE fertility, and with it the population growth, has reached a fairly low level in the industrialised Western World. This becomes clear when we compare Europe with a number of developing countries. If, looking at social-demographic research as it takes place in most European countries, one examines what this tendency means for the family, then it becomes obvious that there is an increasing consensus regarding the number of children one can have. The average number of children in the above-mentioned area varies between two and four, with a modus just under three. Even when considering the wishes and expectations about the future number of children, then one finds a similar tendency towards concentration. These wishes and expectations, though, lie on a ligher level of abstraction. This is especially true if one bases one's research on statements made early in the marriage. Later in the marriage the wishes and expectations tend more to the final number of children. This can be explained by the fact that, at a later date, one has a more accurate perception of one's own fertility. Furthermore there is the tendency to rationalise one's fertility, since one apparently does not like to admit that one would rather not have had children who have already been born.

The actual fertility, i.e. the real number of children, is fully explained by a number of variables. Davis and Blake have, in their classic article, given a comprehensive summary of the factors which influence fertility.[1]

 I. Factors affecting exposure to intercourse (intercourse variables).
  A. Those governing the formation and dissolution of unions in the reproductive period.
   1. Age of entry into sexual unions.
   2. Permanent celibacy: proportion of women never entering sexual unions.
   3. Amount of reproductive period spent after or between unions.
    a) When unions are broken by divorce, separation, or desertion.
    b) When unions are broken by death of husband.

---

1 K. Davis, J. Blake, Social Structure and Fertility: an analytic framework, *Economic Development and cultural change*, Vol. 4, 1955/56, pp. 211–235, p. 212.

B. Those governing the exposure to intercourse within unions.
    4. Voluntary abstinence.
    5. Involuntary abstinence (from impotence, illness, unavoidable but temporary separation).
    6. Coital frequency (excluding periods of abstinence).
II. Factors affecting exposure to conception (conception variables).
    7. Fecundity or infecundity, as affected by involuntary causes.
    8. Use or non-use of contraception.
      a) By mechanical and chemical means.
      b) By other means.
    9. fecundity or infecundity, as affected by voluntary causes (sterilisation, subincision, medical treatment etc.).
III. Factors affecting gestation and successful parturition (gestation variables)
    10. Foetal mortality from involuntary causes.
    11. Foetal mortality from voluntary causes.

A number of these factors are, in talking about developed industrial regions, such as Europe, only of academic importance. This is because, firstly, childless families are not well regarded; and secondly, because the wishes and ideals regarding the number of children show the tendency discribed above.

The factors called "intercourse variables" by Davis & Blake have, as a result, become less important, in direct proportion to the increasingly "universal" character of the marriage, as it is manifested in Europe. The age at which people marry, which in earlier times could be related to the number of children, is also now becoming less important, as can be seen in recent research work. Tabah concludes: "There is no longer any clear relation between nuptiality and fertility: more and earlier marriages no longer make for greater fertility, although the duration of exposure has lengthened. This confirms the fact that couples, and particularly young couples, have acquired greater control over fertility"[2].

It is probable that the weak connection between marriage age and number of children still found as a result of certain research, can be explained by the enforced marriages, which make up a notable percentage of the total. These marriages take place when the couples are still young, when there is certainly fertility.

The other factors mentioned under intercourse variables have little or no influence, in the regions mentioned above. No formal or informal norms exist which could have a bearing on factor 3. The factors 4, 5 and 6 have in our modern industrialised society, little or no influence on fertility, and especially not with regard to the above mentioned tendencies.

The factors mentioned under 7 and 10, connected with involuntary infecundity, have for the most part lost their importance. This is attributable,

---

2 L. Tabah, *Rapport sur les relations entre la fécondité et la condition sociale et économique de la famille en Europe; leurs répercussions sur la politique sociale*, Strasbourg 1971, p. 141.

firstly, to the more frequent and better medical care which limits the influence of these factors; and secondly to the fact that the number of children wanted in developed countries is, on the average, an attainable goal.

The remaining factors 8, 9 and 11 are those which account for the changes and differences in fertility, and which still explain the differences. The influence of abortus provocatus (factor II) has become clear from research[3].

Sterilisation (factor 9) is gaining ground as a method of fertility control. It is furthermore becoming clear from social-demographic research that the various methods of contraception have become common usage in the developed countries. The named variables can still be examined with regard to a number of dimensions, such as the accessibility, the reliability, the application, the degree of effectiveness of the application, and the time when people begin applying the method.

We may assume that the methods which fall under the 3 remaining variables of Davis and Blake, are present in sufficient measure in the region which concerns us; although the various ways may be differently interpreted from country to country 4). This means that differences in the fertility could be explained by the differences between the last 4 dimensions which we named.

Although this is undoubtedly true, one does oversimplify the problem by explaining the differences in fertility exclusively through different interpretations per region and social category, of the distinct dimensions. It is clear from many contributions to demographic knowledge that the possibilities of contraception have been known for thousands of years. This knowledge has, furthermore, been put into practice, sometimes in very effective ways. The early decrease in the birth-rate in France, for example, is explained by a massive and relatively conscientious application of coitus interruptus.

An obvious explanation is therefore that differences in fertility can be explained by the differences in the norms and values concerning fertility. These changing norms and values could have been an inducement for changing one's fertility behaviour.

Although this last explanation doubtlessly possesses a degree of validity, it cannot be said to bring us much closer to the truth. As Kingsley Davis put it jokingly, this is a similar statement to: "birds can fly because they have wings". Further on we will return to this point. One of Tabah's conclusions, in his earlier-mentioned contribution to the European Population Conference, is the following:

"Over the past century fertility in Western Europe has been steadily declining (This is also true for Easten-Europe, B.F.) and seems to be converging within a fairly narrow bracket of between 2.3 and 2.7 births per woman among the generations reaching the reproductive period immediately after the war, declining still further in the most recent generations. The situation appears to

---

3 Ch. Tietze, Induced abortion as a method of fertility control. S. J. Behrman, L. Corsa, R. Freedman, *Fertility and Family Planning*, Michigan, 1969, pp. 311–337.

be growing more homogeneous in terms of space, time and the social hierarchy, as though the family were approaching a model, a standard pattern.

This convergence might suggest to the demographer, especially if he is acquainted with the third world, that the trend is towards a situation of no interest to the analyst. Differences between countries, regions and social classes have lessened to such an extent that it seems useless to discuss them, unless we wish to split hairs",[4]

Some commentary on the above is necessary.

II

The first remark which can be made is that which can be found in the work of Eva Bernhardt. In the introduction to her dissertation, in which she pays attention to the significance of fertility studies in low fertility countries, she postulates: "The general prediction of uniformity in fertility behaviour both between and within countries of low fertility has not, so far anyway, been fulfilled. What then, are the determinants of fertility behaviour in countries where family limitation is widely practised? Although some births are clearly unplanned and unwanted (in fact, a substantial proportion if not a majority of all births may be unplanned in the sense of the timing of the birth) there is substantial evidence to support the view that not only couples want to avoid childlessness, but there is a consensus in all the economically advanced countries on the desirability of having 2,3 or perhaps 4 children".[5]

Secondly: proponents of the stationary population model will immediately point out that it is precisely the difference in decimals which marks the difference between a stationary and a growing population. They too will therefore, in contradiction to those persons who prefer a slowly growing population, choose for an anti-birth policy, for which insight into the rate of birth is naturally a matter of urgent necessity.

Thirdly, the noted points of view assume implicitly that the demographic transition in developed areas such as Europe has been completed. The rate of decrease of fertility is itself decreasing all the time and is showing a tendency towards ceasing altogether, as a result of which the birth to death ratio will remain constant, thus leading to a stable, perhaps even stationary population.

To examine this statement more closely, it is useful to pay some attention to the theoretical background of the transition theory. This is a phase theory, in which the first phase is one where we can speak of a balance between birth and death, although at a very high level. There is strong fluctuation in both figures, the strongest in the death rate. In the second phase the death rate decreases, while the birth rate remains constant. It is obvious that this will lead to an enormous population growth. The birth rate starts to decease in the third

4   L. Tabah, *op. cit.*, p. 140.
5   E. Bernhardt, *Trends and variations in Swedish fertility*, Stockholm 1971, p. 2.

stage, after which a new balance establishes itself in the fourth phase. Here the death rate is far more constant than the birth rate. Developed areas such as Europe would, according to propositions such as that of Tabah have reached this last phase.

If now the demographic transition is defined as the change from a minimal control of the phenomena birth and death, then maximal control would now be a fact.

If one considers fertility, however, one can on reasonable grounds doubt this conclusion. We refer here to the earlier cited statement of Eva Bernhardt. Furthermore, american figures show that a fairly important proportion of the births is unwanted. This same tendency is also apparant from European research. Apparently, despite free access to contraceptive means and a tendency towards stabilising the number of children around three, we have still not reached maximum control of fertility. Furthermore it is clear from the same American figures that about 40% of the births can be regarded as timing failures, something which obviously shows a lack of maximum control.[6] Although we agree with Blake's criticism concerning the material which we mentioned[7], the given figures nevertheless remain interesting, and a challenge for sociologists and demographers. Even if we assume that the control of fertility is maximal, then this does not have to mean that it will stay at the same level. In one of his articles Cowgill forecasts a future population cycle, in which fluctuations in the population cycle c.q. growth are entirely dependent on changes in the birth level.[8] It is apparent from various research that this tendency is not an imaginary one. Since Edin's time (1935) it has become increasingly clear that we can speak of a change in the relation between fertility and social-economic status. The higher layers, which in the past had the smallest fertility rates, are showing an increasing tendency to a relatively higher fertility.

This tendency can be explained by taking into account the changing value attached to having children. Whereas in the past this was in general positively valued, both economically and ethically, today it has become more of an individual decision. One could describe this as a change from the traditional conception of reproduction to a more rational idea. This change has taken place parallel with the often described social change in the same direction. The rational idea which exists nevertheless usually has a completely individual character.

Having children is still positively valued in our culture, and this means that such an individually inspired rationalism could lead to a more or less traditional pattern of family building, moving in the direction of having more children. The U-shaped curve which represents the relation between fertility and social economic status points in this direction.

---

6 L. Bumpass, C. F. Westoff, The "perfect contraceptive" population, *Science*, 1970, pp. 1177–1182.

7 J. Blake, Reproductive motivation and population policy, *Science*, 1971, p. 215–220.

8 D. O. Cowgill, The theory of population growth cycles, *American Journal of Sociology*, 1949, pp. 163–170.

The more one is given the opportunity of realising one's higher demands with regard to fertility through improving one's material position so does the change of a lessening in the decrease of fertility, and even an increase in fertility become greater. This gives reason for suspecting that another phase can be added to the demographic transition, at least, if the individual rationalism which could lead to such a change is not replaced by a more collectively inspired rationalism.

The above mentioned deliberations lead us to the conclusion that there are certainly good reasons for studying fertility in low fertility countries, despite a greater concentration of the figures. Tabah's statement does, however, reveal the difficulties which a demographic researcher must face. It is certainly true that drawing conclusions when the differences in fertility are indicated in terms of one or more decimals is a risky business.

One could therefore question the usefullness of working with "children figures" in this case. Although the analysis of wishes and expectations concerning fertility is done with an eye on the future, the same objection is more or less valid in this case.

The analysis of annual rates must also be regarded sceptically. As Thompson says: "Europe is in fact an area where family planning is widespread. In some countries family planning can be said to be, at some stage in the reproductive period if not continually throughout it, and in some form or other, practised by virtually all couples. And yet, for all that fertility is on average low in any given country, the annual rates remain volatile, comparatively speaking. Why is this and what factor can be identified as explaining large short term variation in fertility but much smaller variation in the longer term?

The answer lies in the spacing of births – the timing of the first birth in a family as well as the spacing of subsequent births – and mainly in the fact that these are now matters on which couples can choose and decide with a high degree of success, given the availability of efficient family planning methods[9]. One can conclude from this that eventual changes in the fertility behaviour can best be tracked down through analysis of the birth intervals. This conclusion is shared by Brass in his paper for the Strasbourg population conference: "direct measures of this (birth spacing) are perhaps the most sensative indicators of trends in family building patterns."[10]

The aim of a thorough analysis of fertility, using birth interval data could be described as the tracking down of changes in fertility behaviour and of the differences which exist between different groupings of the population. This means that, with regard to the changing fertility planning, research must be done as to which categories must be regarded as "go-aheads" and which as "stay-behinds". The results of such a study could then, in the first instance, be

---

9   J. H. Thompson, *Birth spacing data: the new needs*, Strasbourg 1971, p. 1.
10 W. Brass, H. Cillov, *Report on populationdata needs and the use of such data in demographic and social analysis*, Strasbourg 1971, p. 15.

used in the developement of prognosismodels, and consequently as guideline for a desirable population policy.

III

If we assume that the analysis of the spacings, and the differences in them according to social category, can be of use in the solving of this problem of the fertility analysis, and that this can help with the further developement of a theory of the demographic transition, than we have still not completed our task. There remains the question of how to get an optimal result from this analysis.

Earlier we paid some attention to this problem.[11] The result of this was a typology of fertility behaviour. In making an analysis of the Dutch census-material with regard to fertility we will make use of this typology although in a slightly adjusted form. The intervals will be regarded in a number of different ways in this proposal.

In the first place we must regard the intervals, that is the process of family building, transversally. This means that the distinct social categories (religious groups, social economic strata, age categories etc.) must be compared at the moment of counting. This comparison is limited to the sixth interval in view of the relative lack of higher parities in Holland. The tables which are derived in this manner give an insight into the way in which the various social categories built their families, up to the moment of census.

Secondly the intervals are analysed longitudinally, starting from the marriage generations. In this the same variables will be involved as in the first case, although with a less comprehensive categorisation. This method of presenting the data gives an insight into the changes which have taken place within the distinct social categories during the last twenty years.

Thirdly the intervals will be tabulated in relation to eachother. This is done because it has been shown that earlier intervals influence later ones. Differences between the social categories are also examined here. These tables will be used both transversally and longitudinally. (again using marriage cohorts).

Finally both the open intervals and the cumulative intervals will be examined in two sets of tables. The commentary made above also applies here.

The aim of such a thorough analysis is the tracking down of possible differences with regard to fertility between the social categories. As Eva Bernhardt pointed out: "There are however several problems connected with the birth interval method. The two most serious are the truncation effect and the marked variability of intervals which make it very difficult to interpret observed differences in mean intervals. The truncation effect refers to selectivity of women with short intervals in using incomplete reproductive histories. The great

---

11 B. W. Frijling, *Enige opmerkingen betreffende de bestudering van geboorteintervallen*, Utrecht 1969. (Some remarks concerning the analysis of birth intervals). B. W. Frijling, H. G. Moors, Het geboorteinterval in de definiering van patronen van gezinsopbouw, *Mens en Maatschappij*, 1969, pp. 386–395. (The birth interval in the definition of patterns of family building).

variability in the distribution of birth intervals are to a large extent accounted for by involuntary factors (such as pregnancy wastage, and post partum idle period) rather than purposive postponement of pregnancy."[12]

Other objections are those connected with the chosen method of research (the census). A census does not provide information regarding birth control or information on pregnancy wastage etc.

For this reason we must go out from the postulate that differences in interval length are explained by different applications of contraception at the same age. It is therefore assumed that physiological factors have the same influence in the different social categories.

Despite all these objections we still believe that an interval analysis as described above is of practical use. On the ground of earlier research it became apparent that it is possible to see clear differences between the distinct social categories, also regarding the number of children. In the next chapter of H. G. Moors the problem is again examined using concrete research material.

IV. DISCUSSION

If we assume that zero population growth is a matter worth aiming at, this method has several advantages.

It is possible to trace which social categories have still a traditional pattern of family building. In these categories population policy can be aimed at the changing of attitudes concerning fertility.

Furthermore, it is possible to establish which categories tend to exceed the desired number of children. In spite of the dubiousness of the concept we can assume that a number of couples does not succeed in planning their fertility completely. For this category population policy should be aimed at supplying adequate contraception.

These, and other remarks of this kind, also could have been made in the frame of a fertilityanalysis based on "numbers of children". The advantage of the birth interval method is that it is possible to intervene in an earlier stage. In this way a raise in individual satisfaction and a better population policy might be actualised.

---

12   E. Bernhardt, *op. cit.*, p. 91.

Family Planning Patterns:
An Experiment in Describing modern fertility Trends

HEIN G. MOORS*

The Hague

Introduction

THE process of family building is very complicated since completed family size can be the result of differing patterns of fertility planning. One of the main problems of socio-demographic research of human fertility is the estimation of ultimate family size and of the time-span in which this will be realized. Fertility surveys concentrate increasingly on the indices related to ultimate family size. These indices are determined by variables such as "ideal, desired, expected and entended family size".[1]

Hence the practical usefulness of such research depends greatly on the indicative value of these variables. The reliability of wishes and expectations as to the number of children per family, is a strongly controversial topic. Ryder and Westoff evaluated the usefulness of fertility expectations and they came to conclusions which where rather pessimistic in nature.[2]

A small but important step forward shall be gained, if the researcher can succeed in visualizing what his chances are in correctly projecting the individual family growth. Of course, the "actual number of children" functions here as the most important datum. However, our attempt to study the process of family building was also based upon the assumption that the way of achieving the actual family size should be considered as an essential datum. Consequently, a differentiation between actual planning behaviour and fertility patterns will, in this manner, be possible. On the one hand, a typology of this kind should

* Research associate, Netherlands Interuniversity Demographic Institute, The Hague. 15 Bezuidenhoutseweg.
The research was financed by the Netherlands Organisation for the Advancement of Pure Research (Z.W.O.), The Hague.
The data on which this paper is based are those of the Netherlands National Fertility Survey 1969, carried out by the working group on Population Studies of the Institute of Sociology, Utrecht State University.

1 Ryder, N. B. and Westoff, Ch. F., The Trend of Expected Parity in the United States: 1955, 1960, 1965, *Population Index*. 1967, vol. 33, no. 2, pp. 153–168.
2 Ryder, N. B. and Westoff, Ch. F., Relationships among Intended, Expected, Desired and Ideal Family Size, United States, 1965, *Population Research*, March 1969, pp. 1–7.

be highly correlated with the actual number of children, while on the other hand, it should enable the researcher to differentiate among social categories in relation to expected family size.

Changes in the family-building process

As a starting point in our attempt to describe the actual family planning patterns, we based ourselves on three changes in the fertility trends that have taken place in recent years.

First of all one can consider the change in the average size of the family. This is the obvious explanation for a declining fertility rate. The developments in marital fertility in the Netherlands since 1963 can to a certain degree be attributed to this first change.

A second, but an equally important change is the phenomenon that couples who enter into wedlock postpone their childbearing until a later stage in their marriage. Hence the changes in the time table of parentage, especially with the birth of the first child, could have an important influence on the development of marital fertility.

A third new trend is the diminishing spread between the extreme values in the final size of the family. The percentage of families with four and more children is clearly decreasing, however, simultaneously the total number of families without any children and those with one child is also declining. Two causes can be named for this latter trend. As a result of advances in medical science, the application of improved methods of lifting an apparent nonfecundity, has become widespread. A second factor is that couples marry at a much younger age. Fecundity varies with age. As people get older, they become less prolific. Fecundity is already on the decline between ages of twenty to thirty. Although this decline is of no real significance to the lengths of births intervals, the total marital fertility is affected.[3]

With such a development, the average family size may remain constant since the differences above and below the average will frequently cancel out. Nevertheless an influence may well be exerted on the marital fertility.[4] With such a concentration where a large number of families are of the size range of two to four children, the entire reproductive period of a specified marriage or birth-cohort shall be terminated earlier, thus enabling the marriage-births-cycle of the next generation to commence earlier. Naturally substantial differences can arise in the degree in which the three developments, previously mentioned, manifest themselves with different social categories. As a result of the outlined trends the analysis of the relation between fertility and population has become increasingly complicated. Thus in studying marital fertility, it is advisable to take this into account. A first step, hereby, would be to sort out patterns of family building with a social and theoretical relevancy.

---

3 Henry, L., Some data on natural fertility, *Eugenics Quarterly*, June 1961, pp. 81–91.
4 Heeren, H. J. and Moors, H. G., *Gezinnen in Groei*, Utrecht, 1968, p. 14.

An attempt to define some family planning patterns

Two propositions, which link up with the characteristics of modern marital fertility, have functioned as a basis in defining family planning patterns.

1. There is a widespread consensus as to the desired number of children per family – the preferred number being from two to three and at the most four children. This implies that a family will usually be completed sooner, thus enabling the researcher to formulate a projection of the total fertility of a given marriage cohort at a relatively early stage. As starting point for the definition of our typology we used an observation period that was closed after the second pregnancy or earlier.
2. One can assume that there are sufficient possibilities present to enable a stabilization of the family size at a desired level. Hence the application of contraceptive methods and the subsequent result thereof, will form the most important intermediate variable in the actual defining of types of planning behaviour.

We have formulated six planning patterns, using as a basis the preceding propositions as well as the development in fertility described previously.

a) *Subfecundity pattern.* The fertility of the married couple is determined primarily by strict biological circumstances. In this case, planning behaviour is comparatively irrelevant, but it can have distinct variations. This type of family could, in essence, find a place within any of the following patterns.
b) *Traditional pattern.* The married couples have never employed a birth control plan and are determined never to do so, since they object to birth control on moral, ethical or religious grounds. This attitude is generally coupled with large family size desires and expectations, thus actual fertility shall be high.
c) *Hedonistic pattern.* Most of the "enforced marriages" fit into this pattern. The first interval is very short as a result of an unsuccessful contraceptive practice. Even during the second interval birth control is not practiced adequately. The differences between this pattern and the traditional pattern are twofold; the first one being the difference between the two percentages of enforced marriages and the second one being the fact that the couples are inclined to adopt contraception but either may decide to refrain from using it or may decide to use it, but do this ineffectively.
Hence completed fertility shall in fact be quite high among marriages of this type.
d) *Reaction pattern.* The first interval of this planning type is of the same duration as that of the hedonistic pattern. Enforced marriages to a great extent are included also in this pattern. As a reaction to a too short first interval, couples with this pattern thereafter adopt an effective birth controlplan.
Therefore, the eventual fertility shall deviate little from the average type of family building.

e) *Rational pattern I.* This pattern of family building is generally characterized by a short first and often a short second interval in which often no birth control is applied. In those cases where it was applied, this was done during a relatively short period of time. It should be mentioned that among couples following this pattern, there is a conscious preference for a rapid expansion of the family. This is in a sharp contrast with those couples with a hedonistic or reaction pattern. Enforced marriages will not, therefore, occur in this type.

f) *Rational pattern II.* In this pattern couples strive for an extended postponement of the first birth. They succeed in accomplishing this by the effective use of contraception. The second birth interval is usually quite short. In principle the desired family size need not deviate from the average. However, the ultimate family size probably does deviate since couples following this pattern begin to participate actively in the reproductive process at an older age.

By the typification of family patterns it appears that the emphasis has been laid especially on the planning of the first child and on the influence of this on the planning of the second pregnancy. This is due to our conviction that the first pregnancy is a particularly crucial event and of all parities most influenced by social phychological considerations. We agree with Mishler and Westoff's conclusion, that each birth occurs in and is influenced by a different set of circumstances. The sequence of events is viewed as interdependent in that each birth is assumed to alter the family's situation and so effects the probability and timing of future births. The first birth, however, is a point of particular social psychological significance since it denotes the start of the family building process. "The extent to which and the way in which the timing of the first pregnancy fits into the intentions and plans of the couple will undoubtedly influence their modes of reaction to the new situation which has been created and thus affect their orientations toward future births".[5]

Figure 1 indicates the manner in which the differentiated patterns of family building became operative.

Our proposed terminology of planning types has possibly given the impression that we intended to give a characterization of a general mentality. However, our typology refers only to the actual planning behaviour which has presented itself and to the individual's attitudes towards family planning. Social changes will probably lead to new types of family building. Our primary goal was to discover, describe, and to quantify these new types.

The question whether one has learned to accept a specified type of family planning is not relevant to our approach. The issue is not so much whether the planning structure according to which couples build up their family is the real-

---

5   Mishler, E. G. and Westoff, Ch. F., A proposal for research on social psychological factors affecting fertility: concepts and hypotheses, in: *Current Research in Human Fertility*, New York, Milbank Memorial Fund, 1955, pp. 121–150.

no conception within an exposure period of at least 36 months without use of contraceptives			SUBFECUNDITY
never used contraception and not intended to use contraception in the future			TRADITIONAL
did use contraception or intends to use contraception in the future	unsuccessful planning of the first pregnancy	no planning or unsuccessful planning of the second pregnancy	HEDONISTIC
		more or less successful planning of the second pregnancy	REACTION
	more or less successful planning of the first pregnancy	first child wanted as soon as possible or successful planning of the first pregnancy while a short interval was wanted	RATIONAL I
		successful planning of the first pregnancy for at least 18 months exposure time	RATIONAL II

Fig. 1. Schematic Representation of the Family Planning Patterns

ization of an ideal or an adjustment to their situational circumstances. Therefore, it is unnecessary to study first the impact of social, economic and psychological factors on fertility in order to be able to specify which planning type is relevant. This seems to be a rather useless and even an incorrect way of handling the problem.

All these factors only have an indirect influence on fertility.

This does not make it less desirable to analyze differential fertility between social categories, but it is not absolutely necessary to explain fully the changes in the process of family building before being able to determine exactly what these changes are.

The application to a three cohort-sample: Major findings

The defined planning patterns were developed on the basis of the results of an exploratory fertility study that took place in the city of Utrecht, the Netherlands, in 1967.[6]

In 1969 a national fertility survey was carried out. It presented extensive possibilities to test the usefulness of our typology on a larger scale. A longitudinal approach was chosen for this study, based on three marriage cohorts, i.c. 1958, 1963 and 1968. Only first marriages were included with both the husband and the wife of Dutch nationality, while all marriages still existed in the period of investigation. Only wives were interviewed – for both practical and financial reasons. It was expected that all three cohorts together would represent an important phase in the reproductive period, and would show the subsequent changes in attitudes and behaviour with regard to childspacing.

The sample was taken from 67 municipalities which were spread out over all the provinces and included the major cities. The total sample included 3.000 wives – 1.000 from each cohort – and was representative with regard to regional distribution, degree of urbanization and marital fertility, as well as the average number of children and the age at marriage. Slight differences with regard to both the last variables for the 1958 and the 1963 cohort were probably caused by intracohort changes in the course of time.

The response was satisfactory. On 17% of the addresses no interview could be held. 9% refused while for the other 8% the wife could not be contacted because of illness, change of address, etc.

The decision to incorporate three marriage cohorts was based on several considerations. In the first place the structure of the sample would have to enable a retrospective questioning about the reproductive period. On the other hand, the possibility of a follow-up would have to remain open. This was one of the reasons for the inclusion of the younger marriage cohorts in the sample. Furthermore it was possible to compare the 1963 cohort with the 1958 cohort in the same stage of family growth. The three cohorts allowed cross-sectional analyses by interpolation, while the chosen cohorts were expected to give insight into some interesting dimensions of postwar fertility trends. The 1958 cohort represented the slowly changing post-war trend. The women who married in 1963 were the first to have access to a highly reliable contraceptive, the pill. The 1968 cohort would present the most recent information on the changes in fertility caused by the declining age at marriage.

The differentiation of the family patterns mainly took place with the help of the following series of questions:[7]

Q. 25: Some couples are just not capable of having any more children.
As far as you know, is it physically possible or is it physically impossible for you and your husband to have any children, if you want them?

---

6 Heeren and Moors, op. cit., 1968.
7 Parts of the questionnaire we used correspond to the 1965 United States Fertility Study questionnaire.

Q. 40. When did the first/second pregnancy end?

Q. 41. How many months were you pregnant?

Q. 44: Under which of these circumstances did this pregnancy occur?
     (CARD: 1. While not using a method. 2. While using a method and
     did not want to become pregnant at that time. 3. When having stopped
     using a method in order to have a child.)

Q. 34: Did you ever use a birth control method yourself, even for a short
     period?

Q. 52: Do you intend to use a method sometime later?

As a result of the fact that the typification of the patterns was based on a
relatively short observation period of three years or less, the 1958 and the 1963
cohorts could simply be compared with regard to the first five to six years of
marriage. Intercohort changes would primarily show up in the quantitative
significance of the various planning patterns.

Important differences in the behaviour of couples of different cohorts within
a particular pattern would be detrimental to the usefulness of the model. The
characteristic feature of every pattern should be an internally statical datum
as much as possible. The extent to which the speed of family building differed
for the cohorts of 1958 and of 1963 is illustrated in table 1.

Table 1

*The Proportion of Couples Having a First, Second and Third Child Within
Five* Years of Marriage by Family Planning Pattern: Marriage Cohorts 1958 and 1963*

| | First Child | | Second Child | | Third Child | |
	1958	1963	1958	1963	1958	1963
Subfecundity	63	65	12	12	—	—
Traditional	96	100	80	86	21	26
Hedonistic	100	100	89	96	42	32
Reaction	100	100	66	75	18	6
Rational I	96	96	74	70	15	14
Rational II	80	78	15	16	—	—

* The exact period differs from five to six years depending on the month in which the
wedding took place.

There appeared to be hardly any difference between the cohorts in terms of
the percentage of couples who got their first child within the first five years of
marriage. With the hedonistic and reaction patterns this percentage was 100%
for both cohorts; this was a logical result of our definitions. Likewise, this percentage approximates to be 100% for the traditional and rational I patterns.
About one third of the couples with a subfecundity pattern were still childless
after the first five years. There was, however, some shift in the proportion of
couples with a second child within five years, particularily with those who had

a hedonistic or reaction pattern. The percentage of women with a second parity was somewhat higher in the 1963 cohort than in the 1958 cohort. With the third parity a reverse trend appeared. The 1958 cohort displayed, among the patterns mentioned, a relatively larger number of couples with a third child. The overall picture remains otherwise about the same. Couples with a hedonistic pattern showed the highest fertility in the first five years of marriage, followed by couples with a traditional pattern. The subfecundity and the rational II patterns also show strong similarities after the second parity. These similarities can be attributed to two causes. Couples who are in fact subfecund or sterile but do not know this can be credited with having a rational II pattern.

Sterility will only become evident among those couples who have not practised birth control for an extended period of time. Furthermore, couples who have postponed their first pregnancy could have become less fecund. Whether these couples become aware of this depends in both cases on the number of desired children. The determination of subfecundity remains one of the major problems in analysing fertility survey data. Subjective indicators are very often unreliable, while objective indicators can only be established after a long period of time. For all three cohorts, the percentage of women with a subfecundity pattern must display the greatest similarities, since through time there will be only a gradual decline in the proportion of women with this pattern.

One must not expect to find a relationship between certain social variables and the occurrence of this pattern. It is for these reasons that the subfecundity pattern will be left out of consideration in this article.

Figure 2 shows the actual fertility for the cohorts of 1958 and 1963 on the basis of the average family size (the figures for 1969 were estimated).

The process of family building proceeded at its quickest during the first two years among the hedonistic and the reaction patterns. As our definitions have indicated, these patterns are then almost identical in form. After this period, the growth of an average family with a reaction pattern continued at a much slower rate. With the 1958 cohort, the average family size of the reaction and rational I patterns were equal in the fifth year of marriage, while with the 1963 cohort, they were equal in the sixth year. The couples who married in 1958, whose progress could therefore be followed over a longer period of time, have shown as a consequence of the reaction pattern, a fertility level that after the sixth year of marriage was moving quite clearly below the fertility level shown by the rational I pattern. It is not yet certain whether the 1963 cohort will show a similar trend. However, the expected spread of possible future births could make such a development quite plausible.

The traditional pattern shows about the same development as the hedonistic pattern. In the first year of marriage there was an increasing difference in fertility between the two patterns, but this difference seems to maintain itself at about the same level during the years that follow. In the first years of marriage the rational II pattern showed a wide difference in average family size in comparison with the other patterns. The 1959 cohort displayed, nevertheless, that this gap decreased very slowly after the fifth year of marriage, mainly

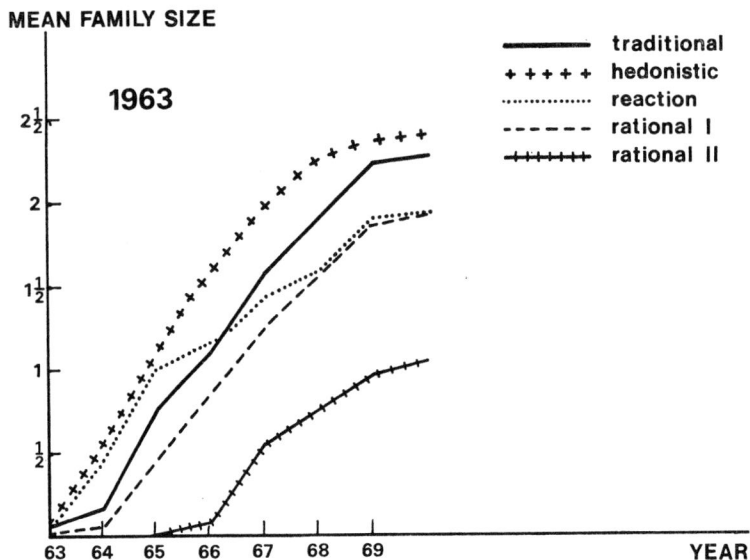

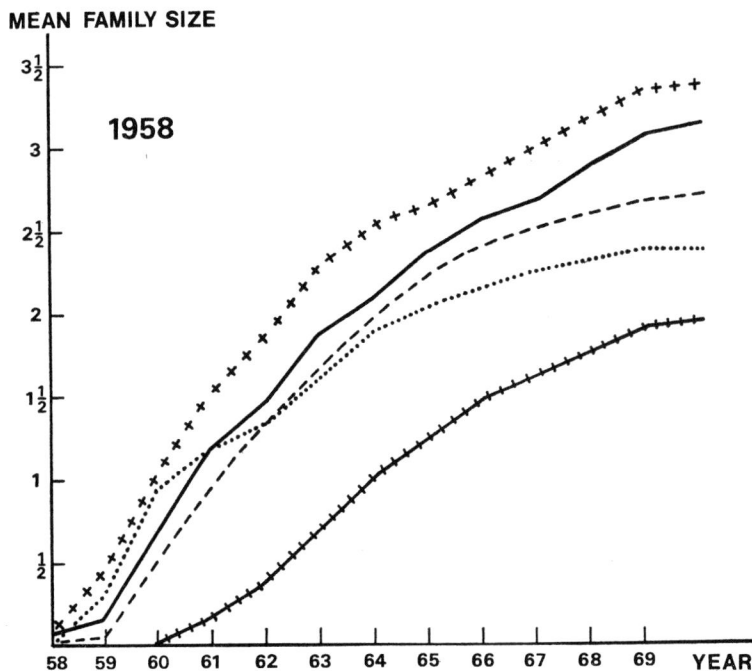

Fig. 2. The Process of Family Building for Defined Family Planning Patterns: Marriage Cohorts 1958 and 1963.

because of a diminishing increase in family size among the other patterns.

Further comment is necessary about the differences in fertility level between both cohorts after the fifth year of marriage. The 1963 cohort has displayed a somewhat higher fertility in the traditional pattern than the 1958 cohort. A greater selectivity within the 1963 cohort in family size values as well as in fecundity is the probable cause. The hedonistic and the rational I patterns among the 1963 cohort show a lower average family size after five years than among the 1958 cohort. An increase in the use of contraceptive methods must have caused this, since in both cases the difference became expressed only from the fifth year of marriage. The reaction and rational II patterns display among both cohorts the same level after five years.

Table 2 divides each marriage cohort according to family planning patterns. Special attention must be given to the 1968 cohort.

The observation period for this cohort was too short to come to a final classification. As a result of this, no impression can be gained of the quantitative size of the subfecundity pattern. It is very unlikely that classifying errors are spread at random over all the other patterns. The classification of the hedonistic and reaction patterns can be considered quite reliable, since there is certainly no question of subfecundity occurring here in the first interval. The three other types of family building are probably not equally well selected. This is especially true for the rational II pattern. Part of the couples in this category will, after an adequate observation period, shift to the rational I pattern. Taking into consideration the total percentage of couples with either a rational I or II pattern and also the division of patterns for the 1958 and 1963 cohorts, it can be presumed that the range of the rational II category has increased among the marriage cohorts after 1963.

Table 2

The Percentage of Couples Married in 1958, 1963 and 1968 by Family Planning Pattern (Subfecundity Pattern Excluded)

	1958	1963	1968
Traditional	13	7	8
Hedonistic	17	17	12
Reaction	9	13	13
Rational I	55	57	44
Rational II	6	6	23
	100	100	100

This increase was coupled with a decline in the proportion of couples with a hedonistic pattern of family building. A comparison of the three cohorts has shown that a growing number of marriage partners, as a result of unsuccesful planning of the first pregnancy, found a place in the reaction pattern, even though the range of the category remained the same for 1963 and 1968. The traditional pattern became less important between 1958 and 1963, after which a stabilization is to be expected for the 1968 cohort.

It is essential here to devote some attention to the various degrees of reliability of our cohort data. The probability of applying birth control, which is a decisive factor in the classification of the traditional pattern, was measured for the three cohorts at different times during marriage. In view of the fact that this variable is subject to an attitude and behavioural change during the course of marriage, the measurement of this variable probably is less reliable for the 1963 cohort and especially for the 1968 cohort. The decrease in importance of the traditional pattern can, in fact, take place more rapidly than can be surmised from the data given in table 2. Explicit family size values were intentionally left out of consideration in our definitions. The whole typology was based on the idea that the way of planning of the first and second interval would have a very great, if not a decisive, influence on the further development of the process of family building and on the ultimate family size. An indication of the final number of children can yet best be gained by means of a series of questions about the expected family size. Table 3 gives an impression of the values and expectations relating to the number of children, as these existed among the various planning patterns.

Table 3

Mean Ideal, Desired and Expected Family Size by Family Planning Pattern:
Marriage Cohorts 1958, 1963 and 1968

	Ideal			Desired			Expected		
	1958	1963	1968	1958	1963	1968	1958	1963	1968
Subfecundity	3,2	3,2	2,8	2,5	2,4	2,8	1,9	2,3	2,7
Traditional	4,7	4,7	4,5	4,0	3,7	3,6	3,7	3,9	3,6
Hedonistic	4,2	3,4	3,6	3,6	2,8	2,9	3,5	2,8	2,9
Reaction	3,6	3,5	3,2	2,7	2,5	2,6	2,6	2,5	2,6
Rational I	3,7	3,5	3,5	3,0	2,7	2,8	2,8	2,8	2,8
Rational II	2,9	3,3	3,3	2,3	2,4	2,6	2,2	2,4	2,5

The differences in both the ideal and desired number of children and the expected family size were the largest between the planning categories within the 1958 cohort. The differences in the category averages of desired and expected family size are smaller when the cohort is younger. It is plausible that all couples, perhaps with the exception of those with a traditional planning pattern, begin their marriage with almost the same desires and expectations of the ultimate family size. However, when their marriage is older, they are often forced to bring their expectations in line with the actual situation at that time.

This process is influenced particularly by the pattern of family building in the first years of marriage. An adjustment in the level of the desired family size will then be effectuated by a process of rationalization.

This is clearly the case for couples with a subfecundity pattern. The averages among the hedonistic pattern indicate the occurence of a similar trend.

The ideal number of children gives a less clear impression.

The differences between the patterns were quite large for all cohorts. As the duration of marriage increases, the different family size values appeared to vary more strongly.

When ideal and expected parity were compared, the differences between them appeared to be the greatest within the 1958 cohort in all patterns, with the exception of the rational II pattern. The difference in the subfecundity pattern is once again most apparent.

A comparison between desired and expected parity shows less marked differences, but here also the eldest cohort exhibits the clearest picture.

The differences in family size expectations between the patterns find their origin only to a small extent in deviations with regard to the desired number of children. This can be observed in the 1968 cohort. If the traditional pattern is left out of consideration, these desires vary in the beginning of marriage between 2.6 and 2.9 children only.

All this indicates that the differences in family size expectations, and indirectly the differences in values also, arise from the influence of the experience that has been gained from planning. This will be further illustrated with the help of a pair of variables, namely a) the use of birth control methods in the successive births intervals and b) the expectations as to the period of time in which the family will be completed.

Table 4

Proportion of couples who used contraception in the first, second and third birth-interval by family planning pattern: 1958 and 1963

	First interval		Second interval		Third interval	
	1958	*1963*	*1958*	*1963*	*1958*	*1963*
Traditional	—	—	—	—	—	—
Hedonistic	4	2	3	1	22	23
Reaction	31	33	100	100	85	77
Rational I	15	15	32	37	37	36
Rational II	100	100	95	82	94	.

Table 4 gives an impression of the planning behaviour in the first three intervals. The absence of any use of contraceptives in the traditional pattern is a result outlined in our definition of this category and therefore requires no further explanation. It should be pointed out, however, that high fertility values are logically incorporated in such a structure. The first interval shows that there exists already in that period a fundamental difference between the hedonistic and the reaction pattern, although this has not yet become apparent in the fertility in that phase.

Among one third of the couples with a reaction pattern there was also found a purposive use of contraceptives as early as in the first interval. The effectiveness with which this occurred was, however, very low and consequently any result is hardly noticeable.

In the second interval – in accordance with the definitions – and also in the third interval, this category displayed itself as a strong rationally planning group with strong similarities with the rational II pattern. As figure 2 indicates, the family size averages appear to approach each other, at least in the 1958 cohort. With the hedonistic type of family building, the proportion of planners was fairly low, even in the third interval. The proportion of planners with the rational I pattern is relatively low as well. We feel that it is plausible that one of the most notable features of this planning type is a comparatively low frequency of premarital sexual activity. This would then be coupled with somewhat conventional child spacing ideals, with which one endeavours for a speedy completion of the family.

However, this hypothesis could not be tested with the material at hand. The couples with a rational II type of planning continued in the second and the third interval as well with the purposive realization of a spacing pattern characterized by relatively long intervals. There is, moreover, a large degree of similarity between both cohorts. Differences should be largely attributed to the small number of couples from which the proportions have been calculated.

All this has obviously its own effect on the time period in which the expected family size will be realized (as illustrated in table 5).

Table 5

The proportion of wives expecting their family to be completed now, within five years or
after more than five years by family planning pattern: 1958, 1963 and 1968

	1958			1963			1968		
	now	≤ 5 yrs	> 5 yrs	now	≤ 5 yrs	> 5 yrs	now	≤ 5 yrs	> 5 yrs
Traditional	50	35	15	14	59	28	1	19	80
Hedonistic	84	14	2	65	25	10	5	53	42
Reaction	81	18	2	51	41	8	6	62	31
Rational I	82	17	1	41	50	9	1	49	50
Rational II	78	17	4	11	84	4	2	37	61

Of course, intercohort comparisons in our survey are rather complicated. The different durations of marriage must be taken into account. The category "1958: now" is then comparable with "1963: now plus within five years". The same possibility for comparisons exists between the cohorts 1963 and 1968, respectively.

Among the 1958 cohort there is only one pattern that deviates from the average i.c. the traditional pattern. Only 50% could be estimated here as having attained the final number of children after a marriage duration of five years. This percentage oscillated around 80% with the other patterns. If we

compare these figures with the proportion of wives in the 1963 cohort who expected their family to be completed after ten years of marriage, then the category of women with a traditional pattern appears to differ once again from all
the other patterns. However, differences are considerably smaller here. For all
patterns there is a higher proportion of couples who expected to have their
family completed after ten years.

Excluding the traditional pattern this can be observed most clearly in the
rational II pattern. The two cohorts display the strongest similarity with the
wives who have a hedonistic planning pattern.

Two explanations are possible for these changes. In the first place, it is
possible that a development is taking place that has resulted in a greater concentration of births among all patterns because of shorter interbirth intervals.

Such a trend could not yet be discerned for the first five years (as in shown
in figure 2). It could also be possible that the process of family building is occuring at a slower speed than actually desired as a result of factors the marriage
partners were not able to foresee. Such factors can be of a physical as well as a
socio-economic nature. This latter explanation will certainly be valid for a
number of married couples. We are not able to determine how large this proportion is.

Social characteristics of the planning patterns

In this paragraph we will attempt to analyse the relationship between the
described patterns and a number of social variables. The usefulness of the typology is, afterall, also dependent on the degree to which the patterns are
socially stratified. "Age at marriage" is an important factor, not only because
of its physiological significance, which is evident, but also because of its sociological relevancy. We can, therefore, expect not only a relationship between
"age at marriage" and the proportion of wives with a subfecundity pattern, but
also the frequency with which the other patterns occur will also differ in accordance with age.

With the 1958 cohort, there was no difference in subfecundity among the
age groups up to the age of 30 years. The percentage oscillated around 27%.
However, 49% of the women with an age at marriage of 30 years or older were
classified as subfecund.

This percentage varied from 16% for the youngest group to 25% for the
oldest group with the 1963 cohort. The difference in level of the 1963 cohort as
compared to the 1958 cohort should once again be attributed to the length of
the observation period.

Table 6 illustrates that there were also important differences in accordance
to age with the other patterns.

When the 1968 cohort is compared with the two other cohorts, it becomes
apparent that among the youngest age groups increasing significance has come
to bear on the reaction pattern.

The hedonistic pattern shows a similar trend while the rational I pattern

Table 6

*Distribution of Family Planning Patterns by Age at Marriage for Women
Married in 1958, 1963 and 1968*

	Trad.	Hed.	React.	Rat. I	Rat. II	Number of Women
— 19 years						
1958	8	38	21	26	8	(53)
1963	6	32	28	32	2	(135)
1968	6	41	47	3	3	(125)
20–24 years						
1958	12	19	8	55	6	(412)
1963	4	14	13	62	7	(471)
1968	9	13	15	39	24	(669)
25–29 years						
1958	14	9	7	62	8	(227)
1963	12	12	5	66	5	(167)
1968	7	9	7	53	24	(168)
30+ years						
1958	38	19	—	44	—	(32)
1963	26	18	5	51	—	(39)
1968	7	7	11	59	16	(28)

has become much less important. This process is difficult to explain. The figures bring us to the conclusion that this youngest age group is, to a large extent, a selection of fertile women. The hedonistic and the reaction patterns are only moderately important within the "20–24 year" category. However, the reaction pattern has increased in significance. At the same time the percentage of couples with a hedonistic type of planning has decreased. Most of the women belonged to the rational I pattern. The rational II pattern as well became very important quantitatively among the 1968 cohort. A similar type of development is shown within the "25–29 year" age group. At the same time there occurred a further decline in significance of both the hedonistic and the reaction patterns.

The women with an age at marriage of 30 years or older present in many respects a remarkable picture. Firstly there is a very high percentage of women with a traditional pattern among the 1958 cohort while thereafter a great decline occurred in this percentage with the 1963 cohort, and yet even more with the 1968 cohort.

The rational I pattern figured here as the most important category quantatively, and there is still some evidence of an increase in this percentage. Although the women with a rational II pattern were absent in the 1958 and the 1963 cohort, they made up 16% of the 30+ age at marriage category with the 1968 cohort.

Striking is the high proportion of women with a non-rational pattern in this age category, as compared with the younger categories with both the 1958 and the 1963 cohorts (57% and 44% respectively). It is plausible that these patterns obtain a somewhat different meaning for the oldest age category. Couples could possibly be aware of a decreasing fecundity and therefore already anticipate upon this in their planning behaviour. In that case it is in fact not quite correct to speak of non-rational-planning behaviour. These couples do not think it urgent to have planning, which aims explicitly at a spacing or limiting of births, since they have reason to believe that biological factors are already accomplishing this. Why such a symptom could not yet be established among the 1968 cohort is not clear.

Socio-economic status appears to be one of the most important variables in relation to the process of family building, In particular, the wife's education had a significant relationship with planning behaviour as is illustrated in table 7.

Table 7

Distribution of Family Planning Patterns by Wife's Education for Women Married in 1958, 1963 and 1968

	Trad.	Hed.	React.	Rat. I	Rat. II	Number of Women
Grade School I						
1958	18	20	7	50	5	(377)
1963	8	17	15	55	4	(344)
1968	9	16	12	49	13	(370)
Grade School II						
1958	11	18	10	54	7	(175)
1963	8	21	10	55	7	(218)
1968	11	9	13	47	21	(294)
High School						
1958	6	12	10	64	7	(115)
1963	6	10	14	63	7	(187)
1968	4	10	12	41	33	(236)
College or University degree						
1958	5	7	11	68	9	(57)
1963	2	21	13	60	5	(63)
1968	1	10	17	30	42	(90)

Generally it can be stated that the rational I pattern occurred most frequently as a type of family building among all the educational categories. There appeared, however, some notable changes over time. The thesis: the higher the level of education, the higher the proportion of women with a rational I pattern, was still valid in 1958. In 1968, however, this trend was completely reversed. Nevertheless, the youngest cohort in particular displayed a rapid increase in the category with a rational II pattern. The higher the educational level the greater this increase. With the 1968 cohort, the rational II pattern was quantitatively the most important pattern among women with a college or university degree.

The traditional way of family building appears to be directly related to the educational level. As this level is lower, the proportion of wives with a traditional pattern is higher. This was especially valid for the 1958 cohort. There was only a small difference between the 1963 and 1968 cohorts in this respect.

There was also a negative correlation with the hedonistic pattern for wife's education among the 1958 cohort. This was less clear with both the other cohorts. For the reaction pattern, little difference could be established between the various educational levels.

The relationship between family planning pattern and socio-economic status was confirmed with regard to other indices such as the husband's occupation and the degree of prosperity of the family. In general, differences were strongest among women who married in 1958, while the 1963 cohort clearly showed all the characteristics of a year of transition. Changes among the cohorts were strikingly consistent.

Religion as well is related with the pattern of family building. The traditional pattern seemed to occur most frequently among the Calvinists: about 20%. Besides, no decrease in this percentage could be established over time. The lowest level was attained by the couples without any religious affiliation: approximately 3% with each of the three cohorts. The traditional pattern was equally important among the Roman Catholic and Dutch Reformed wives. Moreover there were signs of a decrease among both categories.

The significance of the hedonistic pattern differed little between the religious categories of the 1958 cohort. Among the Calvinist wives there occurred a strong decrease in the proportion of those with a hedonistic pattern from 21% for 1958 to 5% for 1968. There was likewise a decrease among the other categories, but this was much less pronounced. The differences between Catholics, Dutch Reformed and those without any religious affiliation were consequently quite small when compared within a cohort. The reaction pattern occurred most frequently in the three cohorts among those without a church affiliation. The other categories hardly differed among each other by cohort.

The rational I pattern was once again the most frequently occurring pattern of family building among all the categories and among each cohort. The proportion was comparatively lowest among those couples without any church affiliation: moreover there was a continued decrease in this proportion from 51% for 1958 to 34% for 1968. The pattern was most significant for Catholic wives of the 1958 and the 1963 cohort. In 1968 there were, however, hardly any differences between Calvinist, Dutch Reformed and Catholic couples.

The proportion of wives with a rational II pattern remained at almost the same level for the 1958 and the 1963 cohorts. Among the 1968 cohort, the couples without any church affiliation differed from the other categories by a rapid increase in this proportion. The percentage of this group that followed the rational II pattern was 31%, while among the other groups it was approximately 19%.

The last variable we would like to analyse in relation to family planning patterns is the size of residence. Four categories of residence were differentiated: *a.* less than 30.000 inhabitants, *b.* 30–50.000 inhabitants, *c.* 50–300.000 inhabitants, *d.* more than 300.000 inhabitants.

The proportion of couples who followed a traditional pattern was largest in rural areas (a). Among the 1958 cohort the percentage was 20% but diminished to 11% among the younger cohorts. The other categories displayed few differences among themselves. The hedonistic pattern was equally significant in the rural areas as in the category d-cities. The percentage was approximately 14% for each of the three cohorts. In the b- and c-categories, 21% and 28% respectively of the couples married in 1958 had a hedonistic pattern. However, in 1968 the size of residence did not cause any differentiation with regard to this pattern. For the reaction pattern the differences were also small. Generally, there was evidence of a decline when the 1958, the 1963 and the 1968 cohorts were compared. Exceptions were the rural areas, where the percentage remained at a low level of about 9% and also the b-category where the percentage for the 1963 and the 1968 cohorts adjusted to the percentage of the c- and d-categories, which was about 17%.

Couples of the 1958 and the 1963 cohorts with a rational I pattern were represented equally among the various size of residence categories that were distinguished. The 1968 cohort, however, displayed a negative correlation between size of residence and the proportion of couples with a rational I pattern.

The percentage decreased from 51% in the rural areas to 31% in the cities with more than 300.000 inhabitants. The rational II pattern presented a different picture. The proportion for the 1968 cohort increased from 16% in the rural areas to 33% in the largest cities. With the other cohorts there were few differences between the categories.

Predictive possibilities of the family planning classification

In the beginning of our paper we expressed the hypothesis that it should be possible in a comparatively early stage of the marriage cycle to obtain relatively reliable indications of the subsequent trend of fertility. In view of the fact that the classification is based on a relatively short observation period, it is relevant to analyse to what extent the classification has had a predictive value for the current and expected number of children at the time of the interview, particularly among the oldest cohort.

The calculated correlation rates (h^2) give reason to suppose that the predictive value of the classification of planning decreased only very little after the fifth year of marriage (row 1). As already clear from figure 2, the differences between the patterns generally maintained themselves. In view of the fact that the eventual family size is realized to an important extent after ten years of marriage, the family planning classification will probably explain about 30%

Table 8

The reduction of variance in predictions of current and
expected family size for cohorts of women married in 1958, 1963 and 1968

	1958	1963	1968
1. Fam. plan. pattern – current family size	.31	.35	.48
2. Original desired family size – current family size	.14	.09	.00
3. Fam. plan. pattern – expected family size	.19	.11	.05
4. Actual family size at end observation period – expected family size	.10	.03	.00

of the variations in completed family size. However arguments can also be advanced in favour of the proposition that this percentage will be higher for young cohorts, because these conform more strongly to the propositions on which the classification is based.

In the first year of marriage, our classification seems in this regard to form a better indicator of actual family size after ten years of marriage than desired family size. It is true that the relationship between original family size desires and current number of children appears to increase in relation with the duration of marriage; however as a predictor this variable is still of questionable significance. It is worth mentioning that the actual number of children at the end of the observation period explained only about 15% of the variance in family size after a period of ten years among the 1958 cohort.

The relationship between family planning pattern and expected family size is at a low level but appears to be stronger when an older cohort is concerned (row 3). This is not surprising in view of the correlation between actual expected family size which also increases with the duration of marriage. It should be noted here that expected family size does not constitute an unchangeable datum and it has actually a somewhat different meaning for the three cohorts. As a cohort grows older, the relationship with desired number of children will decrease. At the same time the degree of similarity with the actual family size of course increases. At the end of the period of family formation there is theoretically a perfect correlation between these two variables.

However, in our opinion a judgment concerning the predictive power of expected family size has to be based on the reduction of the variance when measuring this variable at an early point of time.

The family planning pattern clearly constitutes a better indication than the number of children in the first years of marriage. The differences in variance reduction between the cohorts have to be attributed to the fact that as the cohort grows older, the "reality value" of the fertility expectations increases. This conclusion speaks for the use of our classification along with a concept such as expected family size.

In summary we believe that the conclusion is justified that the family planning pattern classification could be a useful concept in fertility analysis and a useful predictor of ultimate family size.